Becoming an

UNSTOPPABLE

WOMAN

25 STRATEGIES

TO HELP YOU ACHIEVE
THE UNSTOPPABLE MINDSET

Table of Contents

Introduction

She Rises Studios was created and inspired by mother-daughter duo Hanna Olivas and Adriana Luna Carlos. In the middle of 2020 when the world was at one of it's more vulnerable times, we saw the need to embrace women globally by offering inspirational quotes, blogs and articles. Then in March of 2021, we launched our very own Women's Empowerment Podcast: She Rises Studios Podcast.

It is now one of the most sought out Women's based podcasts both nationally and internationally. You can find us on any of your favorite podcast platforms such as Spotify, Google Podcasts, Apple Podcasts, IHeart Radio, and much more! We didn't stop there. The need to establish a safe space for women became an even a deeper need. Women lost their businesses, employment, homes, finances, spouses and more to a global pandemic.

That's when we decided to form, the She Rises Community. An environment strictly for all women about women. Our focus in this group is to educate and celebrate women globally. To meet them exactly where they are in their journey.

It's a group of Ordinary Women Doing EXTRAordinary Things..

As we continued to grow our network, we saw a need to help shape the minds and influences of women struggling with insecurities, doubts, fears, etc. From this, we created a global movement known as:

Becoming An Unstoppable Woman

#BAUW

The movement is to universally impact women of all ages in whatever stage of life, to overcome insecurities, adversities and develop an unstoppable mindset. She Rises Studios educates, celebrates, and empowers women globally.

In this book, you will be inspired by a collaboration between She Rises Studios and

25 phenomenal women from across the globe, as we set to achieve writing a #1 bestseller, "Becoming An Unstoppable Woman".

She Rises Studios offers:

- She Rises Studios Publishing

- She Rises Studios Podcast

- She Rises Magazine

- Becoming An Unstoppable Woman TV Show

- She Rises Community

- She Rises Academy

We won't stop encouraging women to be Unstoppable. This is just the beginning of our global movement.

She Rises, She Leads, She Lives...

With Love,
HANNA OLIVAS
ADRIANA LUNA CARLOS
SHE RISES STUDIOS
www.sherisesstudios.com

Hanna Olivas

Podcast & TV Host | Best Selling Author | Influential Speaker | Blood Cancer Advocate | #BAUW Movement Creator | Entrepreneur

https://www.linkedin.com/company/she-rises-studios

https://www.instagram.com/sherisesstudios

https://www.facebook.com/sherisesstudios

https://www.sherisesstudios.com

https://www.facebook.com/sherisesstudios/community

Author, Speaker, and Founder. Hanna was born and raised in Las Vegas, Nevada, and has paved her way into becoming one of the most influential women of 2021. Hanna is the co-founder of She Rises Studios and the founder of the Brave & Beautiful Blood Cancer Foundation. Her journey started in 2017 when she was first diagnosed with Multiple Myeloma, an incurable blood cancer. Now more than ever her focus is to empower other women to become leaders because The Future is Female.

Living A Life Without Limits

By Hanna Olivas

I believe that we are born into a life with instant limitations, and those limitations can vary from others', from our parents, family members, and society in general. Our parents' beliefs, morals, and values become ours almost immediately whether they are good or bad because of the habitual expectations and guidance of our parents. At a young age, our learned traits begin to define us, but we are always evolving and learning. We will go through life in stages, transforming and building a solid foundation of character and personality. Having fear is inevitable. We all have some, but having fears allows you to grow, and as we overcome our fears, we expand who we are mentally and emotionally, and our limitations lessen, giving us the freedom to expand our growth.

Here are just a couple of examples:

1) If we are raised in a fearful environment, we continue to live in fear.

2) If we're told over and over, "You Can't," chances are, "You Won't."

You may continue to live in fear, but this may also help you overcome it and allow you to step out into the unknown, find some courage, and gain control of your life.

Many people believe that having unlimited finances can lead to a life without limits, but I believe that those are hidden insecurities and that a life without limits starts with a clear understanding of oneself and developing a strong mindset.

One of my own personal limitations was, "I am not good enough" or "I'm scared." It took me three decades and a terminal illness to realize I was the very person hindering my own growth, my life, and my future.

This was a tough one for me to swallow, but self-criticism, accepting and admitting my flaws allowed me to completely change my ways, my mindset, and my entire outlook on life. I needed to find balance, peace, and learn to accept my diagnosis, yet continue to evolve and to do what I love on a daily basis.

Despite my symptoms and how I felt physically and emotionally, I wanted to Become An Unstoppable Woman and Live A Life Without Limits!

I began to face genuine fears and phobias. I started with forgiveness towards myself and allowed myself to forgive others. Life looks different from my eyes now more than ever as clarity and a clear consciousness develops. I had to come to the realization that I had only been existing and I wanted to be living, living a Life Without Limits.

I started to understand my life and its purpose, the meaning of my existence started to make sense and my calling and desire to help others was becoming clear and detailed.

I've since opened a non-profit called, The Brave & Beautiful Blood Cancer Foundation, have become a published author and the co-founder of She Rises Studios in which we celebrate, educate and honor women globally.

For me, learning to live a life without limits meant I had to train myself and condition myself mentally, emotionally, and spiritually. I had to learn to accept who I was and love myself unconditionally. The process was not easy and I wavered several times with doubt, but I knew there was greatness inside of me and I was determined to succeed. I had to battle the demons within. I had guilt, resentments, and my diagnosis almost broke me, but I learned to trust the process and strengthen my resilience and determination muscles because the passion inside me would not let me give up, because FAILURE IS NOT AN OPTION!

I love who I am and who I've become! I am part of the 5am club and this is where I get my zen, the tranquility and peace of the sunrise, the smell of freshly brewed coffee and the gratitude for life and another day. I stand on my bedroom balcony and give thanks to God, I do my daily affirmations and pray for my family and friends. I try to do this daily and I absolutely love doing this because it brings me peace, it's very humbling and it's my way of giving back to the universe and keeping my spirit calm and relaxed.

As women, we face many adversities: depression, heartache, and anxiety, etc. We are also, at times, held to different standards as men, and this can take an emotional toll. This is one thing I never understood, and it can be quite challenging. It is the competition created between women. We use fear and the value we hold within ourselves to judge others, and this is wrong on so many levels. Our own vanity can even be detrimental, causing our perception to be blinded. No matter what challenges come our way, we must always stay grounded and true to ourselves and never waiver from the opinions of others, or their looks or education. We are all uniquely beautiful!

So, practice, practice, practice! Find some techniques that work for you and train yourself to never give up. You must know that every obstacle and barricade is a learning experience and you must be determined to succeed. Your will and desire must always persevere because you are the master of your own destiny. Breakthrough before you break down because You are Unstoppable!

I strongly encourage you to find a mentor or coach to help you develop your skills. This journey has been one shared with many different women, friends, and family. I have sought out opinions, advice and help from others. Please know that you will fail and struggle, but as I mentioned earlier, it is a learning experience and it is about getting back up and in. Set short and long-term goals, get organized, develop a routine, and form positive habits. Create a vision board, use it daily, change it daily and I can't express how important it is to read, read and read. There is so much information and guidance out there. Take advantage and use it as a tool to sharpen your mind to make you unstoppable!

Do not live your life with regrets. Don't be that person who sits around saying "I SHOULD OF DONE THAT". Be a go-getter! The old saying still applies, "CLOSED MOUTHS DON'T GET FED". Start doing what it is you desire, feed your soul and watch the magic happen. I hope you find your passion, your purpose and the strength to chase your wildest dreams. Live a bold life filled with adventure, love and the desire for success. Everything you do should be done with purpose and intent. Live every day like it's your last, every breath exhaled is an opportunity to RISE, LIVE AND LEAD!

That is the beauty of Living a Life Without Limits!

Every day is a new day to live, fight, and conquer. I started traveling more and there are places and things I want and need to see, so I created a "Live it List". Some have asked why I call it a "Live it List" and I explained because "Bucket List" sounds depressing and I'm not done living so, live every day as if it's your last. Get out of your comfort zone, meet new people, take those risks, climb that mountain and share your journeys with the world.

GET GOOD AT WALKING INTO THE UNKNOWN

It's a part of life a lot of us are uncomfortable doing. However, if we step out of our comfort zone into the unknown, that is where life-altering transformations can take place. The more we attempt this, the more our faith becomes larger than our fears. I remember as a child being so terrified of water because of a series of traumatic experiences. As I grew older, I wanted to travel, and I had already fallen in love with the ocean and the crisp, cool, salty air.

It took several trips and me barely even sticking my toes in the water, then one day my husband and I traveled to Florida and some amazing friends made it possible for me to swim with the Dolphins. My favorite getaway now is the beach with the sound of the waves, cool crisp air and the calmness it brings to my soul.

When we open up and share our journey, it allows others to feel your pain or happiness, and it almost feels as if they are there with you, and for some, it can become a healing process. There are people who will be drawn to you or your story, and knowing they are not alone brings a certain calmness. It helps them purge out the negativity and fills their hearts with hope. Remember, if We Rise They Rise!

So, I encourage you to love yourself, love the life you have and create and always try to remain humble. We all have a gift and something to give to someone and there are so many in need of love, guidance and support. Be that inspiration, the encourager and the one who is willing to go the extra mile to give a helping hand. Remember, someone is always watching you and wanting to emulate you, so always hold your head up high, stay focused and true to yourself, and lead by example by being the positivity in someone's life.

Pass it forward, help others and be supportive. Life doesn't have to be difficult or full of struggles. At She Rises Studios, we like to say collaboration over competition. We have a choice to persevere together and create a tribe of grateful, helpful women. Together we thrive, and together we are unstoppable!

Laugh so hard you pee, make memories that last a lifetime, open that business, write that book, take that trip, kiss that dolphin, whatever it is, "Do It and Do It Well"

If you have to Do It Afraid, Do It Anyway!!

From this day forward, promise me, but most of all, promise yourself to Live, Love, Laugh, and believe that you can live a Life Without Limits!

As you read this chapter, I hope you find the strength and courage to Live so boldly that nothing will stand in your way!!

All My Best,
Hanna Olivas

Adriana Luna Carlos

Podcast & TV Host Personnel | Web & Graphic Designer | Best Selling Author | Women's Empowerment Coach | #BAUW Movement Creator

https://www.linkedin.com/company/she-rises-studios

https://instagram.com/sherisesstudios

https://www.facebook.com/sherisesstudios

www.SheRisesStudios.com

Adriana Luna Carlos is a much sought-after expert in Web and Graphic design as well as a new Podcast and TV Host Personnel for She Rises Studios. For over 10 years she has embraced her passion in the digital arts field along with helping women worldwide overcome their insecure idiosyncrasies. Today, when she's not spending time with her family and friends, you'll often find her helping woman focus on rising up and becoming unafraid of success. To learn more about Adriana Luna Carlos and how she can help you overcome obstacles in your business, mindset, or insecurities, visit www.SheRisesStudios.com

The Leader Behind The Scenes: An Unstoppable Mindset

By Adriana Luna Carlos

Finding Your Passion

I was different from most children my age. While most were off watching cartoons or playing video games, I would be racking my brain on how to sell things and earn my own money. I instantaneously had a passion for business and ambitions to be a successful business owner. Growing up, I had a fashion photographer as a father and he loved what he did. In 2nd grade, I was supposed to be in a fashion show as a kid runway model along with my brother. I remember standing on the stage and everything felt so monumental. At the time, I had a fresh perspective and sunk into the grandeur of it all.

The manager of the location explained to my father that the venue did not provide food for the event but that we were allowed to run a concession stand. My father's eyes and mine quickly met because we were thinking the same thing. I immediately told him I wanted out of the runway show and wanted to lead the concession stand. He wasn't surprised, but he kept asking, "are you sure? You can't do both. You wouldn't rather get all dressed up and be on stage? " I told him, "Heck no! I love to sell!! " From that point forward, I was in LOVE with the art of business.

All the customers were getting a kick out of me with my apron on and just taking charge, handling the register, grabbing their food and drinks, and seeing the self-accomplishment in my eyes. It was the most fun I have had to date in my little 7 years of life. I did not care about flashy things or attention from people. I was attracted to having a real challenge in front of me. It was that moment in time that changed my outlook forever and when the brave and young entrepreneur was born.

What is that ONE thing that makes you SO excited that you can not wait to do it each day? What is that ONE thing that you can spend hours researching, learning, and implementing? THAT'S your true passion and THAT'S what you should be doing each and every day of your life. Because you deserve to be happy and doing what it is that you love. If your passion is not already a common position or career, then make it into one! Every single one of us has something special to offer the world that they are looking for and that they need. Perhaps your passion is something completely new to the world and that scares you. My response to this is, you are on to something GREAT and please do not give up.

Settle or Persevere

I've always known that I wanted to help people, and I believe that was the case at such a young age because I was constantly being "messed with." Little by little, I was growing resilience to my situation and to future adversities. Most people do not know, but I had a sexual abuser in my life for 10 years, starting around the age of 5. My family saw that I was constantly angry and was always very opinionated. Looking back on this, I now understand that this was a cry out for help. I thought I was being strong by not telling my family or friends, so this abuse continued until one day I found my voice.

I no longer wanted to be complacent in my moments of weakness and shame. A friend of mine from high school entered my life and, in a way, saved my life. I still remember how our friendship started on the soccer field at marching band practice. I was always a shy kid, so I never initiated conversations, but that was not a problem for my soon-to-be friend. She came right up to me, introduced herself, and asked for my name, and the rest is history. It wasn't long after that, I told her about my sexual abuser and she helped to change my mindset.

Had I not had her support and guidance, my life would be so different. About a month later, I broke the news to my family and I was petrified. The moment I told them, my body was trembling and fear entered my heart but this is a story for another time. Because of this person who took my childhood from me, I became strong and resilient. I grew a new type of strength, voice, and courage to fight through the impossible and make a change for the better. I could have decided to let this troubled time define me, or I could reframe my view of limitations. From then on, I never let fear stop me from finding success. I became determined to conquer my fears and help women find their voices.

In a moment or moments of fear and weakness, find that one thing or person that can help you overcome. You may not see it right away, but you have the ability to push through anything that life throws at you. There's an escape for us all, like music or sports, and that's how you can overcome and persevere. Find what makes you feel INVINCIBLE, because, believe it or not, that will help you get past the obstacle in front of you. These outlets that we all have and use to define us, are actually ways that our brain helps us to cope and prevail. Allow your muse to aid you in building your confidence and resilience, and you will never have to look back.

Reframing Your Limitations

Have you ever been asked in an interview, "What are 3 of your weaknesses?" If so, then you know that the answer they are looking for is not a weakness that you cannot overcome. They want to see if you have limiting beliefs OR if you can turn those weaknesses into strengths. If you are someone who continuously struggles with anxiety, insecurities, or limiting beliefs, then perhaps it is time to reflect and celebrate the growth from your life adversities. Allow yourself to see that you have learned from your experiences and accept these affirmations that you may have unintentionally created.

When I look back at each moment that I overcame impossible situations and adversities, I see new growth and amaze myself. Each life event created new outlooks and built my strength and resilience. I found a voice when I was most afraid to speak up and defend my honor. I followed my passion even when others may not have believed in me. I never allowed myself to be complacent in stagnant moments, but rather, pushed through life's resistance and continued to fight for the outcome I desired.

People can unintentionally make you doubt yourself, but you MUST trust your capabilities and fall back on yourself. Always set boundaries for yourself and others, because if you don't, you will only be living for others. If you can keep finding all the ways to train your mind to be strong, you will achieve an unstoppable mindset.

Do not let all this confidence fool you. I am a shy person and I constantly struggle with imposter syndrome, but I CHOOSE not to succumb to these fears and doubts. Because of my trade, people call me the "expert" and they listen to my every word and they ask for my opinion and advice. It took time to not be afraid to think of myself as an expert, but a lot of what I learned has been self-taught.

I trained my mind to see this dedication as an accomplishment rather than putting myself down because I do not have a degree in my field. You have the power to choose how you identify yourself and your accomplishments. Some of the best advice I can give you is to surround yourself with people who will bring you up in life, who understand your struggles, and who will force you to be accountable for your actions.

You must get comfortable with being uncomfortable if you want to grow and stretch. Never take "no" for an answer!

Finding Your Purpose

I have never been one that wants to be in the limelight. I prefer my comfortable, behind-the-scenes chair because it's where I feel the most power and strength in my abilities. As a web designer, I'm used to being behind the computer screen and not ON it. It's my passion to create moments, ideas and spark emotions through my designs. I believe that you can be and still be a leader even if you struggle with insecurities, doubts, and being seen publicly. "A leader is like a shepherd. He stays behind the flock, letting the most nimble go out ahead, whereupon the others follow, not realizing that all along they were being directed from behind. " -Nelson Mandela

We all operate so differently, but that's what sets us apart and why others will be attracted and magnetized by your unique abilities and outlook. I love making people feel good about themselves, so that way they start to see and believe their worth. I help individuals not let doubts or insecurities mean that they can't achieve even some of the most prominent positions in the world.

Some of you may doubt yourself that if you are an introvert, this means you can not be a leader or that you are not worthy of having a voice. I am here to AGGRESSIVELY state that this way of thinking is WRONG. This is just another limiting belief that you must work on removing from your mentality. Being a leader or role model takes courage, passion, and purpose. You must have a passion for what it is that you stand for, and it's okay if you are not the most outgoing individual. Even extroverts have limiting beliefs and seek help with imposter syndrome. Get aggressive when it comes to fulfilling your dreams and fueling your passion.

Find what makes you happy and see if it is a passion or a hobby. If it is a passion, then explore it and find what purpose it serves you, society, and possibly even the world. Next, find the courage to get started on your mission by finding your support team. There will always be people who support your cause, ideas, and efforts, but you must put yourself out there to be heard. Work on having no fear and continue to stay determined.

Celebrate

Celebrate all the moments, big and small, because they all matter equally. By allowing yourself to accept and celebrate even the smallest of achievements, it gives you a sense of accomplishment and the confidence to move onto the next goal in your life. I believe in positive reinforcement and it promotes a healthy mind.

Perhaps without realizing it, you have always celebrated all the small moments. In grade school we achieved milestones like, "Student of the Week", "Student of the Month" and then we graduated the next year, so on and so forth. Until one day, we graduated from high school, possibly even with honors or as Salutatorian or Valedictorian. All of these small moments allow us to accept and celebrate future accomplishments, like becoming a doctor, opening a business, having a baby or grandchild.

I believe that without acknowledging our efforts, it would be so much harder to overcome the times that we get stuck. We have to provide motivation for ourselves, otherwise we become stagnant in our hearts and minds. Commend yourself as well as others, because they need to hear it just as much as you do.

The Unstoppable Mindset

Perhaps without you realizing it, we just created a version of what an unstoppable mindset looks like! I hope that after reading this chapter, you found something new to take home with you. It was my goal to have you plug in your story into each of these fields to help you see, firsthand, that YOU TOO are UNSTOPPABLE.

Never be afraid to get re-inspired and take action. You deserve happiness and to share with others your passion and purpose.

Find Your Passion, Find Your Purpose, and Persevere! Reframe your limiting beliefs and celebrate all the small and large milestones in your life.

Liz Landeen

Strategy & Action Coach

https://www.linkedin.com/in/lizlandeen

https://www.instagram.com/lizlandeen

https://www.facebook.com/LizLandeen

https://www.lizlandeen.com

https://www.facebook.com/groups/sheconnectsworldwide

After working over 7 years in a leadership level position within a national non-profit organization running multi-million-dollar projects, I left the 9-5 nest to put my strengths and skills to work for myself. I am a Strategy and Action Coach, Founder of SHE Connects Worldwide, and Podcast Host of The Outdoor Entrepreneur. I am passionate about helping women entrepreneurs who feel overwhelmed by all the thoughts, ideas, "shiny things" and mental clutter, to gain massive clarity, and to turn goals into reality with ease and flow. Through my simple yet highly effective Strategy Slay System, I have helped countless women around the globe feel less scattered, more productive and organized, and ultimately on their way to creating an intentional beautiful life by design.

Making Shit Happen and Manifesting

by Liz Landeen

I've made some tough decisions along the way to ultimately get me to where I am today, but for the most part, my story is like so many others. After spending years floating through life, having fun but tied to a 9-5 job I wasn't passionate about, I found myself no longer able to ignore the constant nagging in my gut that was trying to guide me in another direction. After 11 years in my cozy, stable, salaried position, I knew something had to change. What exactly that change entailed was up for debate, but the main message was loud and clear... it's time to get clear, make a decision, and move your ass Liz!

So that's exactly what I did. In 2018 I took some time to figure out what I was good at, what I liked to do, and what I could realistically do as my own business. I even took one of those online assessments to help me better understand what my strengths were. It ended up being a light bulb moment for me and when I became fully aware and tapped into my strengths, with a decreased focus on my weaknesses. I discovered that I value deep connection and building solid relationships, I like order and planning, I'm great at strategic thinking and execution, and I'm impatient for action... WOW, hell yes to ALL these things! It was pretty much spot on. Although I already knew these things about myself, it wasn't until I took the assessment and was face-to-face with the results that I actually viewed them as skills, strengths and assets that are unique to me and what I have to offer the world. This assessment also allowed me to shift my gaze away from what I viewed were my shortcomings, and instead embrace and foster my strengths, because they were what mattered most. Fortunately, my strengths were also largely things I had been doing for most of my career...just not on my terms and not for myself. So, after getting the clarity I needed around my superpowers, I then had to do some deep soul searching and face down a few ugly fears. Once my fears and subconscious mind was properly dealt with, I made a decision, and I set some goals... one of which was to exit out of my 9-5 in 12 months' time. Then, I made a plan, and I worked the hell out of that plan for the following year and guess what? Exactly 12 months later, I successfully left the 9-5 nest and went full time into my own business! It felt incredible, but I won't mislead you for even a minute, it also felt scary and overwhelming at times. What the hell was I doing leaving this incredible job that had supported me all these years? What if this was the biggest mistake of my life? What if I failed and I ended up living on the street with not a dollar to my name? The "what if's" in my mind were constant and loud. But just as loud were the "what if's in my heart and my soul. That gut feeling that gently and lovingly whispered "but Liz, what if you succeed? What if you soar to new heights you never thought possible? What if you build a thriving business that lets you live life on your terms? Why the hell can't you do it! Now go make shit happen and be unstoppable!"

After all the what if's were done doing summersaults in my head, at the end of the day, I always went back to the same thoughts, over and over again... other people are successfully doing what I want to do so why the hell can't I, these are my superpowers and I'm damn good at them, I'm not rushing into anything, I took the time to get clear on what I want and I have a well written plan to get me there, and I'm doing the things I need to do to make it happen... I'm ok and I'm on track...breath girl. I can't tell you how helpful these mental and soul reminders were for me, and I always felt peace of mind and less overwhelmed as soon as I was able to work through my feelings, fight through the fear, self-doubt, and insecurities, and get back to what I know was true in my heart... my success is inevitable, so get on board or get out of the way Liz!

So, I got out the way and I got on board.

That's not to say I don't step in the way or step off the board from time to time... like at least once a day. I always go back to my truths, and I move onward and upward, always.

Just to make sure we're on the same page, I'd like to get this one thing straight with you (in case you feel otherwise)... we have at least one thing in common. Whether you choose to believe it or not is entirely up to you. The universal truth is that WE ARE ALL UNSTOPPABLE...period! Sorry (not sorry) but it's a fact and the sooner we accept it, the better it is for everyone. That's the hard truth, but it's also beautiful, powerful, and freakin awesome! Yes, I know that believing this truth and embodying this mindset many times is so much easier said than done on this roller coaster ride through life and business. Trust me, I get it!! So how about this...at least while you're reading this book, and definitely as you're reading this chapter, promise me, and more importantly promise yourself, that you'll take a minute to acknowledge this truth and invite "I am unstoppable vibes" into your mind and body, even if just for a brief while and even if you don't fully believe it (yet). The objective here is not for us to feel unstoppable all the time, because if we're being honest (and we are) we know that it's not realistic all the time. With the many complexities that come with being human, it's not possible to feel this way all the time. We're going to have bad moments, days, weeks...and it's absolutely one-hundred percent OK. This isn't about "feeling" unstoppable all the time, and it certainly isn't about doing everything right. It's such a cliché but I'll take progress over perfection any damn day...it's the life blood and the engine that drives what it means to not just think and feel good, but to be doing the things needed to BE unstoppable. Like an ocean has water, it's doesn't have to feel, think, or be like water...it just is. We have unstoppable energy pulsing through our veins and built into our bones...it's inherently in us and always there whether or not we think, feel, or believe it. I certainly don't think, feel, or believe it for myself all the time (and no one does). I have more questions than answers, I don't have everything figured out, and self-doubt, worry, anxiety, shiny things, and imposter syndrome are all very real in my world.

So, I take a deep breath, and appreciate the constant duality going on in my head. I appreciate the process of being an entrepreneur and pay gratitude to the journey I get the honor to be on. I buckle up and I get back to living my life and doing the things it takes to get me closer to my goals. I embrace it, allow it to ebb and flow like the ocean, and then I get back in the boat, and get to rowing in the direction of my dreams. The best part is, even though I forget sometimes, I have a freakin life jacket on! It will not let me sink or drown. It always has my back. My "life jacket" are the strategies I use every day to keep me focused, clear, level-headed, and moving forward. These strategies have changed my life and have changed the lives of countless others around the world. This life jacket is what I'm going to share with you so you can put it on, sinch it tight, and have the belief in your strengths and passions to know that you too will not sink, but rather rise to the top, safe, and on your way to wherever you wish. These strategies have brought comfort, calm, and confidence to my life and in my entrepreneurial journey. I hope they will do the same for you (because why the hell wouldn't they work for you too? Oh that's right, they will work for you...yay!!). They're especially perfect for anyone who is looking to make some changes but not sure where to start or for those who feel overwhelmed by how to actually do it. Try them on, see if they fit, swim around for a bit, and have fun knowing that they have your back, just like I do!

5 Life Jacket Strategies (So you can Make Shit Happen & Manifest):

1. *Can I Get a Damn Moment of Silence, Please?*

   With everything going on in the world, the constant noise of social media, and the persistent chatter going on in our own minds, it can feel almost impossible to sift through it all and decipher what's real, what's important, and what's worth listening to. On a subconscious level, we are constantly being talked to and guided, but we rarely listen long enough to hear (or feel) the answers that we deeply seek. Not to mention that being alone with our deepest thoughts and feelings, especially if we're not used to it, can cause us to feel uncomfortable and totally out of our comfort zone. So first and foremost, finding some time to yourself as well as a way to get quiet, is one of the most important first steps we can take if we're looking for insight, clarity or guidance.

2. *Look into the Eyes of Fear & Wink*

   After we've taken the time to get quiet, listen, and get some clarity through the answers we've received, we may then have an "oh-shit" experience. Oh-shit, hell no, are you crazy, you can't do that, who the hell are you to try, don't do it it's too scary and unknown, you'll fail...blah blah blah.

   One of the absolute best things I did for myself early on when I realized I wanted to leave my stable job for the instability of starting my own business, was to do something called a "fear setting" exercise. I learned about this technique after reading one of my all-time favorite books, The 4-Hour Work Week by my amazing boyfriend Tim Ferriss (https://tim.blog/tim-ferriss-books/). Oh wait, I suppose someone should let him know we're in a relationship, lol.

The concept is simple, we must define our fears before we can conquer them. In about 20-30 minutes, this exercise not only helps us to do just that, but it also shines a big bright light on the reality of our situation versus the made up one our mind has crafted. This is hands down one of the absolute BEST things I did for myself, and it provided a constant reassurance and accurate reflection on my darkest days.

3. *Enough is Enough, Decide Already*

Now that we're clear on what we want, and we see that it's not that scary, it's time.

It's time to decide what we're going to do about it. Are we going to stop here and continue on as usual, or are we going to commit to our dreams and goals and the life we deserve and crave? My hope is that we decide HELL YES and commit and fight for the damn life we want. Because you know what, it's fucking worth it (and you're worth it)!! Even if we don't yet fully believe it can become reality for us, or we're not sure exactly how to make it all happen. Or we're scared by the unknowns of it all... it doesn't matter! The bottom line is we CAN have it and we ARE unstoppable, we just simply need to get on board or get out of the way.

Once we've decided it's worth it, we must commit to making it happen and prepare for the long haul. Our dreams are part of a long game, and they don't happen overnight (regardless of what we hear on social media). We can't have long term dreams with short term commitment. So, it's important we treat our goals with the respect, time, and determination they deserve. Decide and commit.

4. *Don't Wing It, Plan It*

Let the fun begin! Now it's time to figure out HOW to turn those dreams and goals into reality. Studies have shown that those who write down their goals are much more likely to achieve them. Can you just wing it, sure. Will it be harder, messier, and produce more anxiety for you...yup! There's no need to feel this way and taking the time to outline a plan of action absolutely helps us to feel less anxious, overwhelmed, and scattered. It will also help us to see the bigger picture, manage our time effectively, be more productive and efficient, stay organized and on track, and be able to make adjustments with ease and flexibility. A plan is essential in the art of making shit happen, especially when we have a long-term vision.

Our goals are the "what" and our plan is the "how." Like driving a car, you know what your final destination is (i.e. your goals), but what's equally as important are the directions to get there (i.e. your plan). A great place to start as you outline your plan is to think about the end result desired, and then how you'll get there by asking yourself "what's the next thing I need to do to move this forward at this moment?" and then keep asking yourself "and then what?" until you've written down all the steps needed to reach your goal.

5. *Dreaming Isn't Doing*

A plan only works if we work the plan. It will only take us so far, and at the end of the day, we MUST implement and do the things we said we would do. Action is queen bee! and it's ONLY through our actions that we'll acquire a whole new vantage point, with a deeper understanding and a fresh level of clarity.

It's imperative to maintain a mindset and an agenda that's rooted in action. Our priority is to focus on progress over perfection, action over anxiety, and done over perfect. When I'm feeling bogged down by something, and I'm having difficulty moving something forward, I get clear on why that is, address it, make changes as needed, and then move on. Because as one of my absolute favorite quotes says, "dreaming isn't fucking doing." It just fires me up! Remember, one of my strengths is that I'm impatient with inaction (my poor boyfriend, the real one, not Tim Ferriss, lol)! But truly, even though dreaming is a major piece to the puzzle and basically the first strategy mentioned above, it's in the doing that we BEcome. This is the ultimate goal, and what I want for me, you, and everyone!

Life is short, even if we have the honor to live a long one. We don't actually know how much time we have in this world (in this present body and form). So, what are we doing being unhappy, unfulfilled, and uninspired? Why are we wasting this time we've been gifted? What is my mind, body, spirit craving? Seriously, sit with these questions for a few quite moments. We say these words all the time but when we really reflect and take in the magnitude of these statement it's a game changer in the decisions we make, perspectives and attitudes we have, and the actions we take.

So, here's the intention I'm setting today and every day, and I hope you'll join me by saying the following out loud and with conviction. Actually, let's scream it from the rooftops! Take a deep breath, get rooted in this very moment, and declare...

- I am NO longer playing small!

- I'm saying NO to limiting beliefs and YES to creating the life I crave and desire!

- I'm saying goodbye to struggle and hello to simplicity, alignment, abundance, flow, and EASE

I'm not here to say that I've reached my pinnacle of success, but I am here to help guide those who are looking to see what's possible when we take time to listen to ourselves, and then SHOW UP for that person as if our life depended on it... because it does! The beauty and power come in the bravery it takes to live a bold life. To live a life that we get to curate, create, and design. To putting in the work and making progress, even when it's messy, scary and our brain is telling us to play it safe, don't do it, you might fail. It's on us to fight back, to find our voice, and to courageously say in response, as long as I live my truth and I am the curator of my life, I cannot fail. I have already succeeded, and I am unstoppable.

Get that life jacket on, jump in the water, and get to swimming my friends...it's an incredible place to be!

Laura Croce

Founder of Laura Croce Christian Business Coaching & Consulting

www.lauracroce.com

https://www.facebook.com/Laura-Croce-Christian-Business-Coaching-Consulting-104768225187976

https://www.linkedin.com/company/laura-croce-christian-business-coaching

Laura Croce, founder of Laura Croce Christian Business Coaching & Consulting, is a successful entrepreneur who specializes in setting up profitable and well-run companies. She believes her Christian values are the reason for her success and infuses them into her business and best practices.

Laura is a certified Professional Life Coach and received her certification from Light University, an External Studies Division of the American Association of Christian Counselors Foundation.

Laura is currently a business coach in Mentor, Ohio. With her business acumen and faith, Laura helps people grow their businesses and enjoy the experience along the way.

Stepping Out In Faith

By Laura Croce

"You can be a secretary," my mother said matter-of-factly.

"But...I want to be in charge!" I replied.

I was young and trying to engage her in another "what I want to be when I grow up" conversation, attempting to explain that I wanted to run a business and be the boss. We would have these occasionally, and being a product of the conservative 1950s era, she would always find a way to dampen my dream. If I said I wanted to be a doctor, she would say I could only be a nurse. If I said pilot, she said flight attendant, and so on. Now, there is absolutely nothing wrong with the professions she was suggesting. She had the mindset that women could "only do certain jobs" and that it would be useless for me to try anything beyond those occupations.

This mindset revolves around limiting beliefs, the thoughts we consider the truth that prevents us from taking further action towards a goal. They can be anything from my mother's view that women could not hold leadership roles, to someone believing they are not creative because their teacher gave them a D on an art project in elementary school. Many of our limiting beliefs form in childhood, often due to other people's opinions and influence. Once created, we tend to cling to these beliefs and stories about ourselves because change can be uncomfortable. If you are challenging the belief that you are not an artist, that means you actually have to create artwork and have other people look at it, and maybe (gasp!) even have it judged at a show. It is way easier to couch surf and not put yourself out there where someone might criticize you. The feelings and thoughts we developed in our formidable years burrow in like a tick, and it can be complicated even to identify what they are, let alone work to resolve them.

29

This is where professional coaching comes in. Someone with a neutral position and a different vantage can really help in pointing out and busting up your personal limiting thoughts and behaviors. I believe everyone can benefit from coaching, and I have been seeing a coach for years now. When my coach and I first got started, we were working on identifying my goals and creating a vision board. These boards catch a lot of flak, but I'm here to tell you that they work. I adorned mine with photos and notes depicting my five-year goals, and I checked every single one of them off the list within two years. If I did not have my coach keeping me accountable along the way, I might still be chugging along on that list, getting in my own way with thoughts and actions that did not serve the future me.

I noticed in my challenges that reframing the situation always helped with busting through negative thought patterns. Rather than looking through the lens of despair, I choose to see roadblocks through the lens of opportunity. For instance, I had many real estate investments at the time of the housing market crash circa 2007. Despite my untarnished borrowing record, I lost almost everything because the banks called back their loans, forcing me to sell at the abysmally low market values. Here are just a few of the limiting beliefs I was staring down at the time:

I do not have enough money to start another business!

I cannot start a business without help from a bank!

The market is terrible to start a business, especially in real estate!

Or had I been blessed with many "opportunities" to pivot and adapt my career? The easiest path was to give up on the real estate industry, but I decided that I would press on, only this time never to rely on banks. You might be thinking this is a bold statement coming from someone with zero money in her bank account, but I knew I would not put that much time or effort into such a flawed system again. I was able to connect with private investors that I had impressed earlier on in my career, use their capital to get my investments back, and I made us all a lot of money in the process. All of this happened on the tail end of the recession.

What are some of your thoughts holding you back from starting the business of your dreams?

I bet I can guess a few...

"Laura, I am too old to start over!" some of you might be saying.

To which I say, no way! Age is an easy limiting belief and an excuse to give up on your biggest and scariest goals. There are many examples of people having fantastic success in the second half of their life. For this, we turn toward Kentucky for our inspiration with none other than the original Colonel Sanders. The Colonel was born in 1890, and his early careers bounced around jobs such as a steam engine stoker to an insurance salesman. Then, the Great Depression hit, swallowing up American businesses and wealth. Instead of throwing away the spice rack, Colonel Sanders developed his secret recipe of 11 herbs and spices as he sold chicken on the side of the road to make extra money. He was just entering his 40s at that time. The first KFC franchise opened in 1952. He devoted himself full-time to franchising his fried chicken throughout the country, and at the age of 73, he sold the company to a group of investors in 1964 for $2 million (which equates to $16.7 million today). Not bad!

"But Laura, change is scary, why would I risk a steady paycheck/job security/my retirement to go for my dreams?"

Change IS scary, but so is living your life at half speed and sometimes, change is downright embarrassing. Take Barbara Corcoran, for example. When the recession hit in the 90s, she had to leave her OWN real estate company to work a salaried job somewhere else to make her bills. She said she was the laughingstock and that everyone around her considered her a failure. Did Barbara Corcoran give up owning a business? Nope, her company survived the recession, and she rejoined at the helm better than ever. "I've since learned that you need to treat obstacles just like opportunity, quickly without much thought and move on." She reported when asked about her struggles. Oh, and guess what? She did all this with dyslexia. Her peers bullied her in school for being "the dumb kid," which she claims motivated her to learn the skills she needed to succeed. What if Barbara believed she was indeed a "dumb kid" instead of investigating why her brain worked differently and figuring out processes to help her improve and study? What if she was too afraid to start buying property and investing in real estate? What if she was too embarrassed to embrace change to adjust her career to be able to last in the long run? Shark Tank just would not be the same!

Perseverance in the face of challenges does not mean fearlessness. I have found it to mean quite the opposite. I've felt a lot of fear as I approached big-time decisions and changes in my life. Perseverance is the ability to do the challenging thing while feeling all the fear but having faith you'll come out on the other side. My faith has made me stronger as I took on significant changes, both personal and professional. My relationship with God has kept me in integrity with all my business dealings, and brave enough to take bold action when the safety net was not always visible (if it was even there to begin with). God puts these passions in our hearts for a reason. They are our gifts, and we honor God by using them. Just because we have gifts doesn't mean that things go according to plan 100% of the time. Businesses go under, and partnerships dissolve. By stepping out in faith, you know you'll have the wisdom to get through any outcome and be able to use your gifts, just maybe in a different way than you intended. We can fail due to our choices, and God can insert a lesson in those failures. I have found God works things out for good for those that seek him. What might seem like a failure to us might actually be a nice little lesson from management "upstairs."

We have discussed the big Goliath-type mindset challenges, but there are also the small, sneaky ones that can derail your goals. These can be just as damaging because they make you believe you are on the wrong path when you are so close to the destination. These smaller challenges tend to pop up after you decide to step out and better yourself. They usually arrive in groups, like gnats attracted to the sweat and hard work you are dedicating to your new life. They typically show up during moments you need to concentrate and not deal with multiple distractions, of course.

I ran into a swarm of these soon after starting my coaching career. I was making sweeping changes, getting websites up, meeting with people, obtaining LLCs and certifications, all sorts of self-improvement activities. On a particularly hectic day, one where there were lines of important meetings awaiting me, the proverbial wheels began to fall off even before I left the house. The spring on my garage door broke, basically trapping my car until I could call a repair person to come on location. While locked IN my garage, I found out my primary email account locked me OUT. This email linked to all my business accounts for necessities like my new website. After hours of back and forth on the phone, the email company informed me that I would have to reset my account and confirm my identity. To do this, they would have to mail me a letter with an activation code. This letter would take 7-10 business days to arrive by what I can only assume was The Pony Express to necessitate that amount of delivery time. A spring had never broken on my garage door, and I had never been so thoroughly locked out of an account that it required a hand-delivered password reset. There I was, just moments after deciding I would take significant action in my life, being blocked (quite literally) from moving forward. If I did not know better, I would have assumed that perhaps I was making a mistake spending this much time on myself or my business or that this was a bad omen for the career path I had chosen.

One of my clients faced the swarm right after we worked on implementing some new processes and strategies to expand her current business. As soon as she started putting the systems in place, orders for that week dropped off. She immediately felt defeated, like something was going wrong. I encouraged her to look at the situation differently and declared that it was a great week for her business. Imagine if she was breaking sales records that week, she never would have been able to implement the new systems we were working on, and her businesses would have suffered later without them in place. God cleared her schedule to make the necessary changes, and she thought this was a sign to pack it up! Having a bad day does not mean your business is failing, nor does it mean that it will be bad forever. Take whatever situation you are facing and use it for fuel. Coaches (like me!) can show you how and put some perspective on the bad weeks and help you appreciate that each new day is a fresh start.

Stepping out in faith is not for the faint of heart. Sometimes, investing in yourself means spending a scary amount of money on intangible experiences. I had the opportunity to take a seminar with Tony Robbins (THE Tony Robbins), and that level of expertise comes with a price tag of about $10,000 for the Business Mastery course. If you have ever started a business, you know all about working capital restraints that many people face, particularly when getting things off the ground. I knew in my heart that I could benefit from this course but coughing up that kind of money for anything less than a car seemed a little crazy. I am happy to report that I got over those limiting beliefs threatening my seminar enrollment. I spent the money, and I made it all back and then some. In addition, I added to my knowledge base all those expert strategies from Tony and his team. It was a once-in-a-lifetime experience, and I continue to benefit from it to this day.

Another bonus of stepping out to grow yourself and your business is passing on success to others. Zig Ziglar put it best: "You will get all you want in life if you help enough other people get what they want." I am incredibly blessed to be a coach and to help people reach their business goals. Once my career flourished, I could pay it forward in ways I would not have matched in previous years. I can now spend my time on non-profit boards and give to causes that speak to me. Because of my successful business career, I can now coach women going through substance abuse recovery and domestic violence recovery through pro bono work and bible study. By filling the pond, all boats rise. I have found more riches in this work than in any business deal, and I would not be able to pass these skills along had I not personally met with success.

During one particularly trying time in my life, my friend asked me what I would do if I only had one year left to live. My response was rather simple: I would not spend another second stuck in my current terrible predicament. I realized then that any one of us could be living the last year of our lives, so why are we wasting any time in situations that do not serve us or are just downright awful? Why do we not step out and have faith that there is greatness just beyond the challenge in front of us?

If this was YOUR last year on earth, what would you change to live a life you love?

Facing these changes head-on is where we become unstoppable.

Nicole Curtis

Kapow Media LLC Founder & Owner

https://www.linkedin.com/in/nicole-curtis-powerhouse

https://www.instagram.com/nicolecurtispowerhouse

https://www.facebook.com/nicolecurtispowerhouse

www.nicole-curtis.com

Nicole Curtis is a wife and mother. She is a country girl at heart and was born and raised in Holland, MI. Nicole Curtis is a Powerhouse Mindset Coach, Women Empowerment Speaker, Social Media Mentor and Author. She is also an Executive Contributor to Brainz Magazine and she has been selected to be featured on the Brainz 500 Global list of 2021.

Nicole Curtis specializes in coaching women entrepreneurs and professionals to become relentless, confident powerhouse women leaders through mindful, personal growth and leadership development. She serves her clients with love and honesty and helps them to step into a new depth of fortitude, self-permission, leadership and expansion. Her business growth strategies are designed to align her client's highest desire with services that will create a powerhouse mindset to awaken their God given power and strengthen their inner voice so that they rise up, beat the odds and dominate as a Powerhouse Women Leader in their life and business!

Choose & Decide

By Nicole Curtis

Hello Gorgeous!

I'm so glad you are here soaking up all the knowledge and information you can so that you might take on a journey for yourself of <u>Becoming An Unstoppable Woman.</u> Before you dive in in this chapter I want to applaud you for taking time out of your busy life to soak up and learn new information that once implemented it literally will change your life, I promise you this!

Today can be a new day for you! A fresh start, a beginning of something magical if you let it, which will not only impact you as a woman but your life, even your future!

How do I know? because once I chose & decided, everything changed for me!

See for as long as I can remember I lived my life to only please others. There wasn't a day that went by where I didn't put my life on hold. I was so busy running around with my head cut off only to feel worn out and energy deprived.

I was so busy pleasing others in my life to feel loved and acknowledged, and worse I devalued myself so much because I was hoping that someone would see me, value me, respect me and validate me!! I was so lost within myself I didn't know how to be myself, let alone know who I was!

I was so entrapped within myself that I filtered everything that I said, even how I acted just to make sure it was ok to do or say so I wouldn't offend anyone or do the wrong thing.

I did this for so long that I found myself drowning in my own pool of brokenness.

Often times I felt like I couldn't breathe. I started to hide, exclude myself from everything and everyone. I would whisper to myself "what's the point in caring anymore!"

I stayed in bed far more than I should of holding the covers close to my face, peering out the window while laying their feeling completely defeated and at times hopeless!

I hated the fact that another day would soon arrive and I just couldn't find the strength and courage to get up out of my safe comfortable place and face the world.

I hated who I was, where my marriage was at, my relationships that I had with my kids and at that time my career.

Yes, I had loved ones who were counting on me, needed my love, attention and support but even knowing that, it wasn't enough to smack me out of the current situation to jump up out of bed and start moving.

I felt completely dead inside! My mind, soul and spirit were broken.

Life felt hard, and I was suffocating.

Days would go by where I felt numb. I was just going through the motions of things, and when I didn't have to show my face or put on a pretend happy smile I was lost completely falling apart.

My mind was filled with an overwhelming amount of lies and stories that I began to believe!

I'm never going to be good enough!

I'm such a failure!

I don't deserve success or to be happy!

No one cares about me!

Nothing good ever happens to women like me!

If right now hun you are feeling these things or saying these things to yourself then I want you to know I hear you, I feel you but more importantly I see you!!

So how did this small town country girl go from all of that to becoming an unstoppable woman who now everyday wakes up being an unstoppable woman?

Who every day picks up her sword, slays her demons and fights for herself, her life and her future?

It is because one day I chose and then decided to fight!!!

It was a cold dreary day when I found myself on my knees, on my bedroom floor, screaming into my pillow with so much rage and anger!

I remember looking into the mirror that was in front of me, with tears streaming down my face saying "Is this really how you want to live?"

Is this really the woman you want to be?

It was in that moment when I heard voices that I haven't heard in a while, I have chills just writing this.

STOP LIVING IN THE DIRT CHILD, GET UP!!!

TAKE HIS SWORD, AND HIS SHIELD!!!

HE NEVER LEFT YOU NOR FORSAKEN YOU!!

IT'S NOW TIME YOU RISE AND FIGHT!!!

FIGHT FOR YOU, YOUR LIFE & YOUR FUTURE!!

YOU WERE MADE FOR MORE THAN THIS!!

GET UP OFF THE DIRT MY CHILD AND SLAY YOUR DEMONS!!

It was then that my whole life changed!!!

It was then that I made a choice and decided to change my life!!

See hun you get to choose how you're going to show up in your life.

You either choose to be a women that shows up in her divine inner power and energetic soul who is filled with complete abundance , self-love and resilience that leads herself and her life or you will choose to be a woman that shows up powerless and broken, who excepts self-limitations and indulges in self-pity and resentment.

It honestly is your call. You are the only one that can choose what kind of women you're not only going to show up as in your life but who you are to become!!

Every morning that you wake up isn't just a blessing given from God but an opportunity for you to choose the kind of woman you plan to live as each day!

You get to be the designer of YOU! You get to choose the path you're going to take, and decide if you're going to rise up and show up as the woman you want to become and live as or not.

You have to create full trust in yourself. (More on this later)

You are the only one that is holding yourself back from becoming your best self!!

You have to get rid of the deep manipulating psychological hold that's in your mind, heart and soul that is keeping you paralyzed in your negative and crappy thoughts and emotions which has you believing that you're not good enough, worthy enough, or even capable enough of becoming such a powerful, unshakeable, and Unstoppable Woman.

Stop letting the words others are saying about you derail you. Don't let your future be dictated by your past, and for goodness sake start running toward what is calling out to you inside, no matter how fearful or anxious you feel!

Don't you think for a minute that you shouldn't answer that quiet voice that has been speaking to you to be more, to want more! To be better, to do better!!!

So the question to you my friend is this…. Right here, right now are you at your breaking point? Have you had enough? Are you ready to rise up, pick up your sword and fight with all your might to grow, change, develop and evolve into becoming an unstoppable woman who wears a crown and not shackles?

If yes, then I want to first say congratulations, you just stepped into owning your power, and I'm so excited and proud of you.

This new path, new road, new journey you are about to embark on however is going to get rocky, bumpy and steep.

I'm just being honest with you right here!!!

You are going to encounter some scary moments, begin questioning if you made the right choice, start doubting your intentions and wondering if they are right, get uncomfortable and some fear is going to set in from the unknown of this new found journey of becoming an unstoppable women and that's ok!

Lean into it anyway, no matter what! Because you are worthy of this! You are deserving of this! You are capable of this!! Second, now that you made your choice, the real works begins because this is where decisions need to be made! Why? because you can't take your crappy self into a bright new future. In order for change to occur, decisions have to be made and I want to help you hun, so I'm going to share with you two personal methods, that is my secret sauces, in which I use on a daily basis that has not only helped me on my journey of becoming an unstoppable woman but living as one every single day!

These two personal methods literally saved me from completely losing myself entirely

1) ESTABLISH A POWERHOUSE MINDSET

2) GIVE YOURSELF PERMISSION

In order to make change, to grow, develop and evolve you have to start the self-evaluation process, and it first had to start with evaluating my mindset!!

I had to become consciously aware, not just how I was thinking but what I was saying to myself!!

I had to change my stinking thinking to powerhouse thinking and it began with the type of words and kinds of tones I was using toward myself.

I had to replace I can't with I can, I'm not worthy with I am worthy, I'm not capable with I am able.

I began to dive into the word of God more for guidance, courage and strength. I allowed my mind to be open to the words I was reading to receive comfort, peace, presence and awareness within my inner soul and heart.

I started writing personal affirmations to myself that I carried with me and wrote down everywhere. Oh, and I didn't care if others saw it or heard me recite them because I chose to go down this new path to get me out of my dark, lonely hole I was in and I decided that me, my life and future was worth it.

I had to call myself out when I would talk to myself negatively or when I was belittling myself.

I had to become my #1 butt kicker!!! I had to get real and honest with my emotions and how I would react towards myself! I started setting small goals to accomplish. I began to get intentional with not just my thoughts and habits but with my energy and time.

I started changing my story of all the things that I thought sucked in my life to things that I was grateful for. I wrote them down every morning, and believe me when I say this, sometime in the beginning just getting one or two written down was hard, but I kept at it every day until it became a habit.

Having gratitude in your life has a way of shifting everything in your life and for me it helped me to replace all the yuck and ugliness I had bottled up inside of me, into something beautiful. It started to create purpose and passion back into my life

I had to become aware of everything that filtered through my mind and do a complete rewire.

Did I receive negative comments and feedback from others regarding all of this? sure did, even from the people that were supposed to love me the most, but I didn't care. I was doing this for me!

A little side note I want to add here is that you're going to have people in your life that once you start changing and growing to better yourself they will start acting differently toward you. Its ok, it's not you it's them because they actually feel threatened by you, because they aren't willing to do what you're doing and their taking it out on you. Just keep plugging away hun, but don't you dare allow them to tear you down!!!!

Did doing all these things happen overnight? absolutely not. Did I have days and weeks where I would fall back into my old patterns and habitats? of course I did, but every day when I woke up was a whole new day in which I got to choose who I was going to be while living my life.

This is why I created a morning mantra, one that I still use today and it goes like this.

"Lord, help me be better today than I was yesterday in all things, in myself, in my family and in my work."

Outside of installing a powerhouse mindset I had to fully and completely give myself permission. I had to stop waiting for permission and asking for permission from others in order to feel love, valued, respected and capable.

With the help of the Lord I had to put me first, and with that came a whole new way of being and living.

I had to change how I was seeking love and dig deep to find it within myself. I had to become self-aware of what I was going to allow and not allow in my life anymore. I created personal boundaries and lived by them daily to protect my energy, my time and my being.

I had to self-forgive myself so that I was able to "bury" the old me so a new me, the next level me could bloom and blossom. I established personal principles to live by and follow so that I didn't get trapped in my old ways of being. I listed out exactly what "I" an unstoppable woman looked like. What I wanted, who did that version of me look like. What did she desire, what were her goals, her dreams and her aspirations in life.

It was in this self-love that I found my self-worth and value and my self limiting beliefs were burned to the ground. I stopped seeking approval and validation from others and found it within.

I had to fully believe and trust in myself! Now I'm going share something with you. Go grab a highlighter if you don't have one handy already or a notebook and pen because this is something I want you to ingrain in your mind, heart and soul!!

You my friend already have everything inside of you to become an Unstoppable Woman!!!! I'm going to say that again, and this time I want you to write it down if you didn't already but insert your name in the blank this time.

I _____have everything inside of me already to become an Unstoppable Woman!!!!!

So I challenge you today as you begin walking in your journey of becoming an unstoppable woman to pick one thing out of both of my personal methods that you are going to right now act on and start implementing today.

Let your inner soul guide you, listen to her she will never leave you a stray. Because when you hear her, answer her call and I promise you, you will begin to live your life in your God given power as a powerful, passionate, diamond queen who slays and fights for herself, her life and her future who claims her inner power and voices her truth!

You are an Unstoppable Women!!

Krystal Vernee

CEO Simply SHE LLC

http://www.instagram.com/i_simply_she

http://www.facebook.com/isimplyshe

http://www.isimplyshe.com

http://www.krystalvernee.com

Krystal Vernee' is a serial womenpreneur, author, speaker and business coach. She owns Divas & Dolls Fitness, a pole and sensual dance studio; Cirque Sensual, a sensual aerial dance brand; Simply SHE, a coaching business and podcast and Krystal Vernee' is her personal brand. An engineer by trade, Krystal knew that entrepreneurship was the ultimate goal early in her professional career. She has always been passionate about creating a safe space for women to unapologetically be themselves and providing the support they need to make the transformation into the woman they have longed to be their whole life. Krystal encourages others to tap into her zone of genius through the Simply SHE Podcast and her coaching program: Passion to Profits. It is her mission to empower women to eliminate self-limiting beliefs and gain clarity in their personal life and business so that they can manifest the life that they desire.

She Wasn't Afraid Of The Fire: She Was The Fire

By Krystal Vernee

Cast out from society, they fed her to the wolves, and she came back leading the pack. When she did not perish, they threw her in the fire, but she did not burn. She stood in her power and simply became it. She is me. My name is Krystal Vernee' and I am a serial womenpreneur, business coach, author, and speaker. I have faced many obstacles throughout my life. Each challenge was unique, taught me a different lesson and helped me learn quickly that I had a knack for leading and thriving through adversity. As a child and throughout my life, I quickly realized that help was not on the way. No one was coming to save me, and it was up to me to change the circumstances of my situation. After continuously being thrown in the fire by family, relationships, career, business, you name it, I had two choices- be consumed by the flames or become the flame, light the way, and ignite others to do the same.

Becoming an unstoppable woman is progressing on your journey to find your purpose and then walk in your purpose on purpose. It took me some time to learn this and discover who I was and what I was truly meant to do. My knowledge and experiences became the catalyst for my transformation not only as a woman but also as a leader, teacher, healer, entrepreneur, coach, and advocate for women empowerment. I want to share my journey with you, the lessons I learned and how you too can become unstoppable. I want to share my Slay Hard Everyday™ methodology.

I was not always this way and did not always have confidence. As a child, I was shy and never spoke up or advocated for myself. I tried as much as possible to fly under the radar, especially when I was at home. My immediate family was raised in the era where "children are seen but not heard" and that was the expectation in my household. My childhood was typical in the sense of going to school, making friends, and having milestone experiences. When it came to my relationship with my mother, my childhood was anything but typical. I believe my therapist called it an "Adverse Childhood Experience" or ACE. I was repeatedly told I was not good enough, I was too fat, too "hard-headed", too grown, too focused on nonsense, not this or not that, the list went on and on. While some may not even be able to fathom the thought of hearing things like this from their mother, these were daily occurrences in my life and would be to anyone growing up with a narcissistic mother.

My mother would often go into these tirades that involved yelling, screaming, her spanking me and resulted in me being in tears. It would be over the simplest thing, and I was taught not to talk back to my elders so I suffered in silence or I would cry. Most arguments were over what I ate or how I was too fat. (Keep in mind, I did not do the grocery shopping as a child so what we ate was what the family ate.) It sounds terrible, but I felt that my tears brought her joy. Her words, "tears don't move me," will forever be etched into my memory. Growing up, I prayed constantly. I prayed for a different family, a different life, a way for me to run away, for God to reveal my real mother, for forgiveness because I just knew I was being punished and for any type of relief from my situation.

Despite my home life, I did extremely well in school. I was a straight A student, with numerous awards and accolades from elementary through high school. Good grades kept my mother at bay sometimes, so I focused hard in school. My mother did not know me then and she still does not know me even now. Performing well in school was the only "thing" I had going for me growing up and I took pride in my work. School was literally my only escape and I wanted to be involved as much as possible. I felt it was my only ticket out of the life I was living. On the outside I appeared to be a normal girl, but on the inside, I was mentally dying. My mother's words cut deep, and I had internalized them. No matter how many times someone told me I was beautiful, I only saw something ugly in the mirror. Even when I brought home good grades, I was cursing myself on the inside because it just wasn't perfect. The mental turmoil that I was going through made it impossible to prepare me for the next nightmare that was coming into my life.

It was in high school that I met my ex-husband. He was handsome, charming, and said all the right things (all the right things that you could say in a "high school relationship" way). While I loathed the way that my mother treated me, I never thought that I would subconsciously seek out the same behavior in a partner. The very thing I was running from, I ran right to it, clung to it and couldn't let go for so many years. We had a tumultuous relationship at best, but no one would ever be able to tell from the outside looking in. I hid my pain and embarrassment very well from the outside world. Now I had two people, the two people that were the closest to me, telling me constantly that I was on the wrong path and that I was living life all wrong. It wasn't that I was living life wrong, it just wasn't how they thought I should live.

As a little girl, I had dreams of having a family, with a white picket fence, large house, dog, etc. I basically wanted what society tells us we're supposed to aspire to have as women. However, I also wanted to be successful professionally and own my own business. I wanted all these things yet; I was told that I had to choose. I had to choose between career/business and family; choose between being a good daughter and good wife; choose between being a good wife and being alone, and the list goes on and on. I was given so many ultimatums that I lost count and thinking back, none of them made any sense. Although none of this really had anything to do with what

I really wanted, I was on a mission to achieve it and on a mission to prove them all wrong.

While with my ex-husband and taking care of my mother, I was working a full-time job and simultaneously building a business. I had fallen in love with the art of pole and sensual dance, and it gave me that spark to live and be true self. What I didn't realize then was that not only had I begun to build a business, I had begun my journey of finding out who I really was and what I was meant to do in this world. I finally felt like I had found my business and my niche and I was determined to be successful. As any entrepreneur that has been in business for any amount of time can tell you, not everything was going according to plan. I was spending more money than I was making, constantly stressed, overworked and desperate for a solution. All I wanted from my ex-husband was understanding that it was going to be difficult, but I would make this studio successful, and it would be great! Instead, I was disrespected, demeaned, mistreated, lied to, and taken advantage of. All I wanted from my mother was respect, to be seen as an adult, and to be the daughter she always said she wanted but I never seemed to live up to those standards.

I gave my ex-husband 17 years of my life and loyalty only to learn that he had been cheating our entire marriage, had accrued major debt and was hell-bent on taking everything I had worked so hard to build. My mother who I had been taking care of, constantly berated me, and told me that she wished she had other children because I didn't turn out like she had hoped. I honestly felt sad, alone, trapped, and just didn't know what I should do. So I paused, I took a breath and really took a hard look at my situation. I had to ask myself if I was truly living for me or if I was living for everyone but me. The answer immediately hit me. It was everyone but me. I knew who I was, I knew what I had accomplished, I knew my own plans and I knew the only thing I needed by my side was God. I decided from that point on that I was going to take control of my life and forge a path ahead of my own choosing, PERIOD. Out of sheer desperation, anxiety, stress and success, the 7 pillars of the Slay Hard Everyday™ (SHE) Methodology was born.

When I really sat back and reflected on all my experiences, I realized that in order to overcome each challenge, I was following a set of innate steps. These steps had been perfected overtime as I learned from new experiences, helped others, and had to make important life decisions. I realized that for the SHE Methodology to really be effective, one had to have clarity on who they were as a person, their goals, vision, values, etc. and they had to surround themselves with positive people. That was really the foundation for everything. When I lost myself in trying to live for and please everyone else, I lost sight of who I really was. It therefore became easy for me to believe the lies that I was being fed. It was so easy to internalize what they were saying because the people doing the most harm were so close to me and I figured they knew me more than anyone so it must be true, right? I just did not have the confidence at the time to take a step back and stand up for myself. Therefore, this led me to the first pillar in the SHE Methodology- The BOSS Identity™.

The BOSS Identity™ stands for the Best Observation of your Subconscious Self. It focuses on you standing in your power and defining yourself, your core values, beliefs and who you are. You formulate your BOSS Identity by using words to describe yourself, activities/actions that you do well, what matters to you and who you are. I then use "I AM" statements to affirm what I KNOW to be true. My BOSS Identity™ Statement is as follows: I AM an intelligent entrepreneur who breaks boundaries and serves her community; a confident woman who empowers women and seeks to positively change the world; a creative teacher who inspires others to achieve self-mastery; a fierce advocate of self-love who teaches self-care and embraces spirituality; and a fearless coach that sets goals, plans, and gets results.

The second pillar of the SHE Methodology is defining your Circle of Influence™. One of the most influential factors that affect you is your circle, the people that are closest to you and that you spend most of your time with. Your Circle of Influence™ consists of 3 layers: Inner (closest to you), Middle and Outer. Your Inner Circle should be filled with like-minded people that encourage you to be better, create a balanced relationship, are trustworthy and respect you. Your Middle Circle will have people that are probably acquaintances, there may be some commonalities, but you may have less things in common and they will present themselves as inconsistent. The Outer Circle people will be consistently negative, critical, lacking in vision, untrustworthy, unsupportive and bring about turmoil in a relationship. I felt stagnate for so long because I was conflicted about who was in my Inner Circle, who had to be in my Inner Circle and who wasn't in my Inner Circle. The key point here is that regardless of relationship (e.g., family, friend, etc.), everyone has a place in the Circle of Influence™ and just because they are family doesn't mean they get to be in your Inner Circle. I felt the greatest sense of relief and grew the most when I came to terms with the fact that my mother and my ex-husband were in my Outer Circle.

The third pillar is Blocking Out The Noise which involves releasing self-limiting beliefs and ensuring to carve out time for yourself. Everyone should practice self-care and self-love. It is not selfish to take time for yourself and you cannot pour from an empty cup. The fourth pillar is setting SMART Goals. SMART Goals stand for Specific, Measurable, Attainable, Relevant and Timebound. I am a project manager and everything centered around goals, milestones and deadlines so I thought, why not practice this in my own life. Making a list of the things you want to accomplish and the deadline is the first step. Ensure it relates back to what you ultimately want to achieve (e.g., buying a home, starting a new relationship, etc.). Then, list the steps you think you need to get things accomplished and take action. I know this is easier said than done but overtime, if you make it a habit to take action, you will move closer to your goals.

The fifth pillar is the Power of Manifestation. If you believe that you can accomplish something, you will achieve it and if you don't, then you won't. Be intentional about calling good things into your life all the time. Don't focus or dwell on the negative because it happens. You can't choose what happens to you, but you can choose how you react. I choose to react in a way that will result in the highest good for me and those around me. The sixth pillar is BOSS Habit-building. It takes 21 days to create a habit and I really had to look at what habits I had and what habits I wanted to create. If I had habits, such as spending too much money, that would result in negative consequences, I did whatever I could to break those habits and instill new ones that would put me on the path I wanted to travel. The seventh pillar is BOSS Decision-making and one of my favorites because I learned that this is a teachable skill and one that I'm passionate about. There are never right or wrong decisions, but each decision has different consequences. One must make decisions based upon their own unique experience and information that is presented at the time. I have found that I would often stress over decisions, but what I learned is that your life experience prepares you in the moment for what is to come. None of us know what challenges we may be faced with or how many times in life we may be thrown into the fire. However, using the SHE Methodology in your own life as I have used it will help you Slay Hard Everyday.

Natalie Pickett

Entrepreneur, Speaker, Mentor

https://www.linkedin.com/in/natalie-pickett-74b00910

https://www.instagram.com/natalie_pickett_mentor

https://www.facebook.com/nataliepickettmentor

https://www.facebook.com/groups/livingthedreamcommunity

http://nataliepickettmentor.com

Natalie has founded multiple businesses, with both 6 & 7 figure success stories. Refreshingly honest, Natalie shares insights into her triumphs and so called 'failures'. Along the way, discovering, that becoming unstoppable, is less about hard work, and more about finding joy in your every day. As a mentor, and speaker, she shares her knowledge of how to take your business, and your daily life, from surviving to thriving. It is possible to define your own version of success and easily take the steps you need to achieve your goals. It is possible for you to, not just Dream the Dream, but Live the Dream. Passionate about sharing this with the world, Natalie shows you how in her chapter in this book, and in her Living the Dream online course.

Living The Dream

By Natalie Pickett

When you ask someone if they want to be living their dream life, it is unlikely that the answer would be anything other than 'yes' but what does that actually mean?

'Living the dream' became my catch phrase one summer afternoon. My siblings and I were sitting in the Australian sunshine, drinking champagne and eating shrimps (which we call prawns). We looked at each other and said out loud that we were 'Living the Dream'. Whatever else was happening, it didn't matter. Right at this moment, we were living our best lives.

I've always loved business. Even as a young girl, I used to convince my friends at elementary school to play 'business' with me. I'd be the head of some corporation, or I'd convince my siblings to play 'shops' with me, and I would work out each item's profit margin. People think that a 'business mind' is different to a 'creative mind', but when you can create something where there was nothing, that's creative. Turning an idea into something bigger, such as a business that benefits everyone who buys from you, is undeniably creative.

I started my first business when I was 28 years old. My 'office' was a little study annex off our bedroom. I still remember the excitement when the first bookings came through and the excitement when you receive sales never goes away.

Even though I had already been living a dream life, it took a major shift to get there. Sometimes things need to end so that you can start new beginnings. There are some very commonly used phrases, such as 'everything happens for a reason', and 'what doesn't kill you makes you stronger'. While there can be a lot of truth in both, sometimes it is difficult to reconcile with the actual experience. Sometimes things happen, tragedies, that you just can't fathom how you could create a reason for such a thing. When I was 19, my boyfriend of three years was killed in a car accident. He was the driver, and three of his passengers were also killed. Not only was I mourning his loss, but I also had to accept that he was responsible for three other deaths. At the time, I wished I was in the car too. I had said I would be there, but for some reason I decided to stay home. Maybe it was destiny, maybe it was intuition. As fate would have it, had I been in the car, the front passenger (who I would have been) was the sole survivor. I don't know what could have been worse, surviving because I made the decision not to go out, or being the sole survivor of such a devastating accident.

I rarely share this story, and even though it happened 35 years ago, I can still feel pain in my heart. Anyone who has experienced grief of any kind will know that it takes time to feel okay again. It's like you function on autopilot, you're a shell of yourself and not fully present. I remember someone asking if I was 'over it' now. It is something that we ever 'get over'. It is something we learn to live with.

We all get to tell our own story, but often our story is reflected back to us externally. As I found my way trying to 'get over' his death, I realized that people don't know how to deal with you. Some people avoid you, or avoid mentioning his name, and in others you see the look of pity on their face. Arriving at events like engagement parties and weddings on my own, people would sympathetically pat my hand, and tell me that I would eventually find someone else. His death had defined me, as this person of tragedy.

If I was to search for reasons as to why this had happened, now I can say that our time together was complete for his lifetime and I remain grateful for the love and life that we shared. At the time, my coping mechanism was to close my heart and move on with my life.

Our patterns of behavior and coping mechanisms, usually formed when we are children, are so strong, and this strategy of closing my heart possibly helped me cope through childhood challenges like my parents' divorce. Patterns are useful to protect us as children, but to become an evolved adult, you realize that they no longer serve you.

A turning point happened when I was involved in a car accident that same year. I was stationary at a red light when I heard a loud noise. As I looked in my rear vision mirror, an out-of-control truck was careering towards me. I thought I was about to die. I clicked off my safety belt and slid under the steering wheel. I watched the roof of my car on the driver's side slowing being crushed by the weight of the truck, which eventually caused my car to roll on its side. Miraculously, I survived, and the paramedics suggested I was so lucky that I should buy a lottery ticket. I took this as a sign that I was not meant to die yet. I was meant for more.

No longer wanting to be defined as the 'poor young widow', I felt the urge to make a leap. An opportunity came to move to the Gold Coast, in Queensland, on the east coast of Australia. Family friends had offered me work in their bikini shop, which sounded like a fun departure from what was my current career in banking. I could create my own story, a new story that wasn't defined by the past.

While the job in the bikini store didn't work out, I soon found work as a waitress in 5 star restaurants and resorts. These were exciting times. It was the late 1980s, and tourism was booming. I was single, young and free. My motto was, 'if it wasn't fun anymore, I wouldn't keep doing it'. On my brief visits home, my friends and former colleagues at the bank would often respond to my new adventures with 'wow, I wish I could do something like that'. Incredulously, I would reply 'but you can!'. It's about choices, but not everyone can see the choices or know how to take steps toward living their dream life.

I then travelled to work in the Whitsunday Islands and then Cairns, both on the beautiful Great Barrier Reef. Between work, I would snorkel, SCUBA dive, paddle board and waterski in this tropical playground. I had also achieved my Fitness Instructors certificate, and using Cairns as a springboard, I left for the US, the UK and then Europe. In the US I worked as a Camp Counsellor, and in London I began working as a Tour Leader, leading tours throughout Europe, where for two winters I was also a Resort Manager based in the Swiss Alps. I gained further management experience based in the London office, responsible for managing tour operations, road crew, and training new tour leader recruits. It was a great life, but for anyone who has lived a transient lifestyle for a long period of time, eventually you yearn to 'put down roots' somewhere, and I had started to miss being home. If it wasn't fun anymore, it was time to move on. By the time I returned to my hometown of Melbourne, I had been away for more than 7 years.

During my time as a tour leader, I was fortunate to lead some VIP tours bringing travel agents from Asia to Europe. Sydney had just won the bid for the 2000 Olympic Games, and they told me how popular Australia was becoming as a travel destination. Just as I had been as a young girl, I became excited about the idea of starting my own travel company.

My business specialized in bringing international visitors to Australia, and my clients were the overseas travel agents who sold Australian holidays to their clients. I quickly outgrew my home office, and rented office space nearby. I had a strong reputation for success, and I was asked to speak at conferences, chair industry association boards, and I was invited to be a tourism awards judge.

To look at me from the outside, I was running a very successful, multiple 7 figure business. I would be hosted to stay at 5 star resorts in Australia, and travel the world on sales trips. My partner and I also decided to get married in the beautiful little village where we had worked together in Switzerland, and our fairytale wedding was followed a few years later by the joyous birth of our beautiful daughter.

As perfect as it all appeared, I wasn't happy. I used to wake up almost every day, and this feeling of sadness would envelope me. I felt like crying. Me being me, I would muster the strength to get up, put on a happy face and go through my day.

It felt like there was something missing, and like many business owners and moms, I was often running low on energy.

Eventually, I came to realize that I was busy prioritizing everybody else my family, my husband, my business but I had lost sight of me. I wasn't looking after me. I had allowed a pattern to form in my personal relationships and my work life, where I would always put my needs last. I would get upset with my husband because he didn't seem to prioritize me. The light bulb moment was when I realized "how could I expect anybody else to prioritize me, if I wasn't prepared to prioritize myself?" I hadn't been paying attention to my own emotional needs. I was "achieving" based on some external list and my feeling of success related to other people's opinion of me.

I learned the hard way that it's so important that you prioritize yourself first, otherwise you will just drain yourself. No one else can do this or advocate for you. I had been giving and giving to everyone else but hadn't allowed myself to receive.

The tourism industry is subject to many external factors. You can be hit with something overnight, such as unforeseen natural disasters, pandemics, acts of terrorism and economic downturns. Suddenly, people stop traveling and your cashflow vanishes. Even though I had managed my business through so many of these disruptions for 15 years, the 2007–2008 Global Financial Crisis was too big to survive. I was also going through a difficult divorce involving financial and custody disputes.

Everything came crashing down. As much as this was a crisis, it was also an opportunity for me to create the life I really wanted. On my own terms. I had forgotten my motto. I had forgotten to make sure I was still having fun. This is my Phoenix story. Everything had to fall away, because the structures that I had built were not serving me. If you follow the tarot, The Tower card shows everything crumbling and falling to the ground. This was my "scorched Earth" moment, and although it looked like I had lost everything, the things that really mattered were not lost. My daughter and I were both safe and well. Today, I am cognisant that the current pandemic is a similar time. No one knows what the future holds.

I also understand and appreciate that everything had to crumble in order for me to start again. My "The Tower" card trigger was when I found myself searching for support whilst on a trip to Queensland's Daintree Rainforest. I tried something new. A chakra or energy healing, and a "spiritual alignment". After the first session, the healer told me that my heart chakra wasn't just broken, it was smashed to smithereens. I suddenly understood why I was waking up every morning wanting to burst into tears.

During the spiritual alignment, there is a process to align with your spirit to discover what you truly want. I was so blocked energetically that I hadn't been allowing my intuition to be open or available. Words like "forgiveness" came up. "Who do you need to forgive?" my therapist asked. Of the people on this list, I realized the most important person that I needed to forgive was me, not for anything specific but I understood that forgiveness for myself was paramount in me moving forward. The same for trust, not just trust in others but mostly trust in myself and letting go of fears around emotions. Refreshed and renewed after this session, I started to work towards creating the life that I wanted to live.

Divorce and business closure proceedings can be energy draining, and soul destroying. My strategy, was to take one day, or sometimes one intense hour, at a time. One day, a friend called me. I was on my way to a custody mediation session and negotiating terms for the business closure at the same time. "OMG, are you okay?", he asked. "I know from the outside that my life looks like a train wreck," I replied, "but in the middle of it all, me as a person, I am okay."

I told my friends that this was not something I was "going through, but something I was growing through." I learned that in vulnerability you'll find your true strength. Being brave is about honouring how you feel and being true to that. Taking time to ground yourself before entering high pressure situations will have you negotiating with a clear sense of purpose.

Change can be messy, but so worth it on the other side. When you are in the middle of "the muck", you need to be pragmatic and tend to what needs to be done, but don't focus on "the muck", turn your attention to something good. I created a game to do with my daughter called "3 favourite things." Each night at dinner we would list at least three of our favourite things for the day. The favourite things can be simple, seeing a beautiful bird, or sunset, enjoying nice food, or time with family or friends. Savouring these precious moments in the day helps you to refocus your thinking on positive moments. Even on the darkest days, there is always things to be grateful for.

You may be amazed to discover that within months after everything crumbled, all of the things that I had imagined in my aligning with spirit session, had manifested. I was living in my dream home. I had a 6 figure consulting, speaking and mentoring business.

I worked part time hours, prioritizing myself and time with my daughter. I woke up feeling happy each day.

It took quite a journey to discover that Living the Dream is less about working hard and more about following your joy. Make decisions with an open heart, be guided by your intuition, and prioritize yourself. I now work with my clients and in all of my businesses sharing that passion.

Sara Martinez

Head Retreat Specialist

https://www.instagram.com/smspecialtyevents

https://www.facebook.com/groups/2601808560149852

www.smspecialtyevents.com

www.retreatleadersmastermind.com

Sara Martinez is the founder of Retreat Leaders Mastermind and all-around business badass. She has been a dynamic force in the event world for over 17 years, rallying high-vibe female entrepreneurs to take control of their businesses and re-ignite their purpose through transformational events. A visionary since the beginning, Sara's passion as an event planner stems from a deep desire to be the droplet which creates an empowering ripple throughout the entrepreneurial world, bringing together women and creating connections that leave an impact.

Part-event planner, part-author, part-yoga teacher, and part-adventurer, Sara began her early career in corporate & nonprofit meetings, but eventually followed her heart to create SM Specialty

Events, a small-business-minded event company, and most recently launched Retreat Leaders Mastermind (RLM) with partner Jennifer Andino. RLM brings together several elements that the retreat sector lacks: accessibility, first-hand experience, a VIP done-for-you service and a wider-than-wellness focus. Sara and her family love to travel, hike, spend time in nature, and she is currently in the process of writing her first book. Join Sara at the Retreat Leaders Mastermind Facebook Group https://www.facebook.com/groups/2601808560149852!

Discovering the Women Within

By Sara Martinez

Unstoppable women: some are born, others are taught, but all are capable! For me, becoming an Unstoppable Woman was destined, taught, and created through the culmination of life events. My journey to become unstoppable started with Discovering the Woman Within.

I grew up in the suburbs of Chicago, and even though my family had financial struggles, we never went without. My father always pushed me to be the best, in sports, in school, in life and I never allowed myself to disappoint him. On one hand, this taught me all that I can achieve. On the other hand, I learned and internalized limiting beliefs around scarcity, perfectionism, and self-worth.

In stark contrast, my mother was always hustling to keep her 4 children, her husband, and everyone else happy. Unfortunately, this often came at the expense of her own happiness. Watching her, I learned perseverance in struggle, but as I became an adult, this also manifested as an exhausting responsibility for everyone else's feelings. Mine, almost always, came last.

You see, from the moment we are born, we experience social conditioning. Through every moment in our lives, we are taught to look a certain way to be loved, live a certain life to be happy, and have certain things to be successful. We are taught to conform. What a load of crap!

Yes, I said it. It is a load of crap. You know why?

Every person on this planet is unique. Each has unique capabilities, a different way their brain processes information, a kaleidoscopic look and all are beautiful. All are worthy of love, and 100% of women are capable of becoming Unstoppable. The masculine hustle culture is detrimental to the creative, feminine flow inside of us!

In the United States, we have a culture that says to be successful you must be in a constant hustle state. Do you know what happens to those that are? Many end up burning out. Others go through midlife crises'. Some never achieve that happy life they so desire. This is why the hustle mentality must go. Becoming an Unstoppable Woman is about finding harmony by going within, discovering the woman who has been kept quiet, and letting her shine. Only then can you be truly Unstoppable and create the life of your dreams.

I joined the hustle lifestyle when I became a competitive gymnast at 5 years old. This meant long hours at the gym, training after school and nearly every weekend. That wasn't enough for me, I craved more. I began playing baseball/softball at the age of 8, and then soccer for a couple years around that same time. Factor in playing travel softball in my teens, and it was clear: my brain had been wired to hustle. I was changing outfits in the car, grabbing fast food, doing homework in between, and convincing myself this was what I had to do to earn success. Isn't this what many adults are doing today?

Now, don't get me wrong, it was fun while I was in it. We traveled often for competitions, I grew a friend group that existed all over the country, and I learned to love playing on a team. I was always trying to learn more, be the best, and was constantly going! These behaviors served me for a time, but eventually, their usefulness faded away and they started inhibiting future growth. That's when I had to confront them head on.

I carried this hustle into my adult life, and my tremendous momentum continued: I graduated early, moved out with my (now) husband at 17, and I began working odd jobs. Soon, I took a job with a corporate meeting planner. This was the inception of my career, I was successful *and* enjoyed it! At 19, I started a charity for Dogs with Hip Dysplasia, and I spent many of my weekends working events to raise money for the non-profit. Then, I started a construction business with my husband where I took care of all the project management while he did the on-field work.

Then we had our son, and life again took a huge turn!

Motherhood is a lot like other things in life: we think we know what we want based on what others around us are doing, but often, we realize (once we are knee-deep in the hustle) that we want it to look different. I had planned to work the construction business from home, to be home with my son, Logan. Due to my own limiting beliefs about what it meant to be 'valuable,' this new work-from-home dynamic was a difficult adjustment. It brought me into a phase of my life where, when I think back, all I see is darkness. I was so lost. I didn't know what it meant to be 'me' anymore. I had lost my hustle. I had lost my identity.

This was the awakening for me. This is where I realized all the social conditioning I was inundated with, from the circumstances that had surrounded me all my life. I was a collection of everything that had ever happened to me, as well as the survival tactics I used to weather my path but now I was in uncharted territory. I had no idea who I was, what I wanted from life, or what made me happy. In my work today, I see so many women in the same place, at 20, 30, 40 and even 50 years old.

So, what did I do? I meditated. I don't remember where I first learned about it, meditation was still new to me. However, I quickly found a place of calm that my body enjoyed, and one day, an intuitive message came to me: the next step was yoga teacher training. I needed to know more about this calm, and I needed to share my newfound discovery! I had discovered my intuition and was beginning to listen to her. There was a local studio I envisioned as the catalyst of my new yogic learnings, but they didn't offer any teacher training. I spoke my intuitive desires out loud to my husband: that I wanted my training to take place at this specific studio, the one my heart felt drawn to. The next day, what pops into my Facebook feed? that studio! Plus, my dream mentor announced their new offering: an upcoming teacher training. I was in!

This training was one of the best experiences of my life. I questioned everything about myself. I found a woman within me that I didn't even know existed. I felt so in tune with my inner self that it was almost overwhelming. During my training, I felt the incredible force of yoga, union to source, throughout my entire life.

The end.

Not exactly.

I kept up with a lot of it after the training was over, but the hustle mentality returned. Social conditioning got back in the way. This isn't an overnight process. It is a lifelong commitment to that Woman Within.

My training led me to discover retreats, and I fell madly in love. I discovered why disconnecting was so essential to deeply connect with one's truth. At first, I was the one attending retreats. But with each one, I realized that *hosting* retreats was what I was made for. Another business was born, SM Specialty Events. I launched my first Moms on Fire Retreat in Tucson Arizona in 2018, and over 40 women attended. Their transformation stories proved I was right where I belonged.

My husband and I still owned Cutting Edge Remodeling, and it was doing well. Life continued to get fuller and in 2019 we welcomed our baby girl, Harper. We had two businesses, two kids, a dog, some chickens, and a heck of a lot of stuff. Then Covid hit.

This was the first time in life that I had to do something completely foreign: just *be*. Pretty damn uncomfortable for many of us, considering our social conditioning. At this time, I was heavily considering shutting down my business. I was still in the beginning stages of SM Specialty Events, and the first few years of any new business are always a heavy investment in time and money. I sat with it for some time, while my husband urged me to keep going. In that moment, he saw what I couldn't: I was made for this work. Eventually, I came to see it too: the work and sacrifice and waiting were worth the women's lives that were being changed through my retreats.

As I reflected during the shut-down, I found that I hadn't lost my passion, but I had again lost myself to exterior opinions of what my business "should" look like. As a people pleaser, I was taking on everything that I could, and at that point I wasn't just hosting retreats, but I was offering planning, logistical and other retreat services to small business owners. It wasn't the way I felt most called to do it, and it wasn't aligned with my soul's purpose. I continued to meditate, and got close to my center, so I could more easily recognize what was in alignment, what was authentic to *me*.

Once I had a clear answer, I set boundaries around my professional services, and became more intentional about which clients I would bring on. Almost immediately, I started attracting that same shift in my business. During that time, I also manifested my business partner, Jen who was a stranger to me until we were brought together on social media! First, I was managing all of her retreats in Costa Rica, but that quickly evolved into creating a retreat together.

That solitary retreat transformed into the single focus of my business. It grew like wildfire because it is purely in alignment with the reason I started my business: to make an impact in the world, and watch real women's lives transform for the better. The women around me were beginning to see how magnificent they were. Hosting a retreat or two a year was great, but my vision had always been bigger without the dreaded side effect of 'hustle.' Now, I get to work with women who are authentically themselves, who have great gifts to share with the world, and I get to help them to create retreats to impact even more.

This ripple effect is the bigger vision I had, but years ago couldn't pinpoint.

Not only has this clarity allowed me to create the impact I desired from life, but it has helped me to travel more which, I learned in meditation, is a deep desire of the Woman Within me. Alignment also has me currently questioning so many other areas of my life. I keep getting a loud and clear message to sell everything and travel; my eyes are open to all the "things" we have accumulated over the years: cars, boat, RV, pool, hot tub, a house full of items, most barely used. Why do we do this? Why do we hustle and hustle and hustle, just to buy things that sit?

When we open our eyes, we see that it is not the *things* that bring us happiness, but the experiences that those things create. So often, we believe that because the person next door, or the mom on social media seems happy, our brain subconsciously believes once we have that, we will be happy. To become an Unstoppable Woman, don't seek externally. You must go within.

Are your beliefs yours or did they come from someone else? You must go within and find your soul's purpose. Once you find that, you can then determine how to fulfill that purpose to have harmony and synergy within your life. You must truly know yourself, before you can fully be Unstoppable. You must question all that you know to be true and decide what is true to *you*. True to that unique woman within you. Question each layer of your life and the beliefs that create it.

- What home life do you want to create?

- What do you want your relationships to look like?

- What are you doing for work and what is the impact you are making?

- What do you create financially and how are you prosperous?

- What does your daily life include?

- What do you want to leave behind?

- What material possessions can you release in order to open up room to fulfill your true self?

I believe having mentors in your life is a huge part of becoming an Unstoppable Woman. Whether it be a marriage counselor, parenting mentor, business coach, or other guide, don't forget to be curious about the advice of a mentor. Decide if it is in alignment with the desires of the Woman Within. Is it authentic to your mission and overall goals for your life? Is it authentic to your heart? If it is not in alignment with the vision you have for your life, or authentic to your beliefs, it doesn't matter how great the advice is, it has the potential to take you down a path that is not your own. For this reason, enlist mentors that share your values around life, money, family, and business. When bringing people into your circle, remember to bring them in because they inspire you, not because you envy them. Envy will steal your uniqueness and authenticity. Inspiration will bring it out!

As you read through this book, you will find an array of amazing women that are experienced in different areas of life. Finding a mentor should be much like hiring a nanny, someone for your business, etc. Find someone that resonates with your beliefs.

For the next few months, why not try these strategies and see if you feel closer to the Woman Within? Remember, each woman is unique and being an Unstoppable Woman will look different on each of you.

1) Drop comparison. As long as you are comparing yourself to others you cannot discover the Woman Within and live a life authentic to you.

2) Choose an area of your life you want to increase your fulfillment in

3) For the next month evaluate this area of your life:

   a. In this area, what parts are working?

   b. What beliefs do you need to question/re-evaluate?

   c. What needs to be let go?

4) Utilize strategies from the other authors or tools that are you already have to dive deeply inward, like:

   a. Meditation

   b. Journaling

   c. Hypnotherapy

   d. Praying

   e. What allows you to disconnect from the outside world, and reconnect with your inner voice?

5) Make changes based on what you discover

6) Rinse & Repeat

Using this will help you to Discover the Women Within and from that you become Unstoppable! Becoming an Unstoppable Woman is within all of you! It will not happen overnight and it is not about the destination or finish line, it is about enjoying the journey of discovering that woman, honing in on her authenticity and honoring her!

Valerie Carrillo

Real Estate Professional

www.linkedin.com/in/lasvegas-valerie-carrillo-6bba214b

www.instagram.com/livinglasvegasig

www.facebook.com/NormaValeriaCarrillo

I am a wife, mother, friend & social butterfly. I focus on empowering women by educating them on the process of home buying and providing resources and professional connections to help them reach their goal of home ownership. I host fun quarterly events for home buyers to answer any questions they may have. I've created "The Woman's Guide To Owning Her Dream Home," which demonstrates the step-by-step process that takes the guesswork out of how to get started. This year 2021 marks 20 years of being in the Real Estate/ Finance industry.

Love, Truth and Being a Female Warrior

By Valerie Carrillo

I grew up in Las Vegas Nevada. My parents bought their first home here when I was five years old. I still remember our first night in our new home. My mom bathed my little sister and I wrapped towels around us and laid us in front of the television. I was starting kindergarten the next day and I was very nervous. We had very little furniture that night. But I remember we had nice big tv. There we were my mother, myself and my little sister all huddled together and I think about that night a lot. My childhood was a happy one and very family oriented. I had twelve aunts and uncles and lots of cousins. We played outside every day and our aunts would take us to the lake on the weekends. My aunts bought a home just a few blocks away and those years were some of the happiest times.

I started babysitting when I was twelve years old. They were a great family and I consider the parents I babysat for my second parents. Even after I got a job at a fast food place they were always there for me. At fourteen I went to an orientation my older sister had for a new fast food restaurant opening across the street from our home. The manager offered me a job and with my sister next to me I quickly jumped at the offer. A couple of weeks after my sixteenth birthday I was up early in the shower. It was the day I was picking up my schedule for my junior year of high school. I heard my mother yelling my fathers name. I rushed to get a towel and run out to the living room. She was doing CPR on him. He had had a heart attack and died in his sleep. We all fell apart. I had a rough junior year. My older sister decided to move out and I went with her. I knew I was going to need a better paying job, so I applied at the same casino she was working at. I worked six pm to two am and had class at 7am. I worked that schedule my junior and senior year and was proud when I graduated high school.

The month before my twenty-first birthday I had my first child, Sophia. She was the most beautiful baby I had ever seen and I was in love. When I turned twenty-one I became a cocktail server. Two years later I had her brother Daniel. We had our girl and our boy and we took on the goal of home buying. We worked hard and saved our money and at twenty three years old we got our keys and were so proud. Through that process and with the guidance of our agent I was inspired to become a Realtor. In 2001 I received my real estate license. A few months into our new home we found out I was pregnant. Our youngest and the baby Gabriel was born. I had three kids age four and under. That was a rough time. I was still working six pm to two am and had to be up with the kids in the morning. I was blessed to have my mother in law come stay with us on and off from California throughout the year. When she wasn't with us my mother would help out. I remember one afternoon I was exhausted. Sophia and Danny were fighting and Gabriel was crying. My then husband was at work. I couldn't take it anymore and I was crying and frustrated. I called my mother crying and she came right over and picked them up. I slept for hours and I was so appreciative of the help. It was a rough, rough time. During our time in our home we paid off our cars and all of our debt. Things were great.

Five years in our new home and the kids got older, we decided to upgrade our home. We sold our first home and bought our second home. It was a beautiful home with a pool. We had a savings, three beautiful healthy kids, owned our own cars and besides our home we were debt free. Again, things were great until they weren't. All of a sudden, our credit cards were maxed out and our beautiful home was in foreclosure. A few weeks before it was going to be sold on the courthouse stairs at auction we were able to find a buyer and were forced to sell one hundred thousand dollars under value. I decided to leave my marriage. I started 2006 as a single mother with three kids. Heartbroken, frustrated and exhausted, times were tough and I was struggling. I got a job as a secretary during the day, bartending at night and was working my real estate business when I could. The next few years took a toll on me. I had to step up and do what I had to do for me and my kids.

Divorce proceedings started and the real estate market crashed. I felt I just couldn't catch a break. In 2008 I met a nice young man 8 years younger than me. He was single, never been married and had no kids. Here I am in my thirty's with 3 kids. We talked and talked and talked. We started dating and I fell madly in love. I loved the way he looked at me. He was the only man that I let meet my children.

My ex moved to California with his parents and I let the kids go see him over the summer. Right before school started he called me and advised me he was going to enroll them in school over there and he was not sending them back to Vegas. I was so upset. I hung up and told my boyfriend what had just happened. He quickly told me to pack a few things and he insisted on driving me to Northern California to pick them up. The custody battles began and it became overwhelming. Court hearing after court hearing and it was so difficult and stressful. My boyfriend started picking up the kids at my mother's when he got off work. He would bring them home and help them with their homework.

I remember one night coming home from dinner and the boys were asleep in the backseat. He carried them both in, took off their shoes and put them to bed. I watched and his actions were putting my heart back together. I couldn't stop staring at him and how he cared for my kids. He was so genuine and playful my kids instantly fell for him. I had completely fallen for him. That night as we laid in bed I stared at him and asked him why. "Why what?", he said. Why do you want to be with me? I'm older than you with three kids. My tubes are tied and I can't give you a child. Why? I will never forget that moment. He looked at me and stared into my eyes and in Spanish said, "porque eres una guerrera, una guerrera para tus hijos y te quiero mucho". He said "because you are a warrior, a warrior for your kids and I love you very much." I think about that conversation often. His words did more for me than he will ever know. Throughout our years together when he catches me sad or upset and things just aren't falling into place, he reminds me and says, hey "adonde esta esa guerrera?" where is that warrior I fell in love with? With those words he gets me out of my funk.

We got married and set some new goals for ourselves. Real estate was picking back up and his construction business took off. We were doing really well and we were very happy together. Sophia finished high school and shortly after Danny finished high school. Gabriel was in his senior year in high school and I felt blessed to have a career where I made my own schedule. I was able to watch him play baseball and go to his wrestling matches. I always made sure I was very involved in their education and sports. Sometimes I would take him lunch to school and we would eat in my car. Those hours were very special to me. Soon he would be 18 and leave the nest.

Once Gabriel graduated that June, I decided to throw myself full time into my career. The last half of that year I did well. February of the following year I decided to hire a business coach. I needed a strategy. I started hosting first time home buyers workshops. I remember my first one I was so nervous I started sweating I actually thought I was going to throw up ha ha. It turned out great and that was the first of many. That was something I had never done. My coach made me go out of my comfort zone. I hosted several over the summer and my business took off! That fall of 2019 I was in Las Vegas Woman magazine in the Real Estate Leaders section. What an accomplishment that was for me. I couldn't believe it, big things were happening for me. Clients were coming out of the woodwork. It was a great year and I hit over six figures. October rolled around and we moved into our beautiful forever home. Even though it was my best year ever, it was still very hard for me to celebrate my accomplishments. My broker would hand me my check and say, aren't you happy? I'd say, sure.

In the back of my head, I knew I could still accomplish more. I knew I could be more productive. I thought and knew I was still slacking. I was feeling lazy every day. I now had two out of my 3 kids out of the house. Things were going so well but I was depressed. I felt exhausted just waking up in the morning. I knew that wasn't me and it went on for a while before I realized it. I decided to make an appointment with my doctor. She ran all kinds of tests and we found out I was severely anemic which I knew my entire life but I now had an auto immune and she thought it was Lupus and wanted me to have more tests done. The entire time I hadn't been feeling well and being hard on myself I was really sick. It wasn't me and what I wanted to accomplish throughout the day but it was my body. My body was stopping me and hindering me from the things I needed to do. Once I understood that, it was a whole new ball game. I pushed hard from wanting to be in bed all day. I pushed hard when I was exhausted. I was not going to let Lupus beat me.

December came and my daughter, Sophia the oldest that is always by my side and had been my assistant for 3 years was moving out. I took that real hard. She moved out December 1st and even though I was proud I got depressed again. I cried all of December. The first 2 weeks I cried myself to sleep every night. All month I was in a crying state. January came and we heard on the news about the death of Kobe Bryant and his daughter Gianna. Here came the waterfalls again.

That was all that was on the news for 2 weeks. Finally, my husband had enough and did everything he could to pull me out.

March came around and Covid hit. What a mess and disaster that was and still is. Suddenly, I was having deals fall apart left and right. My buyers started losing their jobs and were unable to qualify for the homes in contract they were in. My sellers were unable to show their homes to qualified buyers if the home being sold had tenants in it. We couldn't force a tenant to show the property per Covid. The next few months besides work my husband and I stayed home. We were only allowed trips to the grocery store. We couldn't go places if we wanted to, businesses were shut down. Month after month we stayed home. Once businesses were able to slowly open up again, we still waited a couple of more months.

Fall came around and I knew I needed to get back to my A game. I hired my business coach once again and we started to strategize for the last quarter of the year, I wanted to finish strong. I met with her once a week, so I knew I was being held accountable. I started new campaigns. I started to hold quarterly events for my clients and also for my neighborhood. I hosted an awesome Halloween event in my cup de sac. I knew I had to become the Realtor in my neighborhood. No way did I want to see someone else's sign on my street. I was running email campaigns so my neighbors knew I was here and could give my expert advice. I was listening to some awesome motivating podcasts and reading all of the top books. I've been through a lot and I feel like it is a sad story but I realize it's not. I've had to struggle at times but knowing what I have overcome has given me strength. I'm still here. I'm still standing.

My friends and family have been a blessing and I appreciate them very much but in the end I have to be strong, for me, for my husband, my children and my family. My story has a lot of love. I love without limits. I'm a hopeless romantic. I'm sharing all of my truth. This is me. I'm sharing how I got the word Guerrera (warrior) engraved in my mind, body and soul. I'm sharing how I pushed through. Some days are easier than others but like my first mentor and broker said to me 20 years ago, "Get up, Dress up and Show up"! Mr. Ed Shuman would look at me and say "Manifest Destiny young lady!" Those words I never forgot and I am forever grateful he cared about me and took me under his wing. This year marks 20 years in the Real Estate/Finance business for me. Being an empty nester, hiring a business coach and finding out about my auto immune has taught me so much about myself. My mental health and self care are so important to me now. I have set some new goals for myself and have a plan in place to live my best life. I am most excited to share it with my loved ones.

Love, Truth & Being a Female Warrior

Michèle Kline

Growth Consultant

https://www.linkedin.com/in/michelekline

https://www.instagram.com/micheleklinekhc

www.klinehospitality.com

Through intentionality and dedication, Argentinean immigrant, Michele Kline built a career in the Hospitality Industry, "playing chess and not checkers". Seeing the bigger picture and adeptly anticipating several moves in advance.

She founded Kline Hospitality Consulting LLC, a successful firm focused on helping businesses and professionals grow, providing the industry with tools to improve the quality of its services, financial performance and the growth of those professionals invested in it. Specializing in Process Improvement, Brand Standards & Image Assessments, Management & Board Advisory, as well as Coaching, she is also known as "a fixer".

A respected Leader, expert in building customer-focused Teams, as a result of her advanced knowledge in Human Resources & Employee Relations. Michele has a personalized and hands-on approach. In 2018, she was granted the Learning & Development Professional of the Year award by the Nevada Hotel & Lodging Association, apart from other recognitions throughout her career. She passionately strives to inspire others and promote collaboration.

Win or Learn!

By Michèle Kline

Dear reader, my name is Michèle and I am a quiet and humble Ninja Warrior of my own life. I decided a couple of years back, when I turned 40 to be precise, to be my own Hero and instead of wearing a cape, I choose to wear stilettos, lipstick and quite often, my hair in a ponytail. Stilettos, because I strongly believe that life is a party and we should dress accordingly. As embarrassed as I may be to recognize this, lipstick is part of my superhero daily outfit because I consider myself a one-step-girl and as such, that is as much makeup as you will most times see me wearing. I don't know what it is about ponytails, I just feel they get me in a "get things done" kind of mood. Ok, I just got side tracked, back to it...

You know how on TV talent shows, each participant is introduced by a compelling story about their life struggle? Touching, melting and rehabilitating those hearts of everyone glued to the other side of the television. As I start writing, I come to realize how many stories of my own I could share with you today. To give you a quick sense of perspective, I just made a list and oh boy do I feel overwhelmed now.

The story of my life starts with my adoring Family comprised of Mom, Dad and my big Brother. I LOVE THEM! We are a tight clan and TO THIS DAY, consult everything with each other... yes, everything. When I was in kindergarten, I was tasked to draw a picture of my Family. It was colorful and detailed but... my Dad had no legs! That was my first experience dealing with suffering. My Father had been in a car accident. This tragic event made him an even stronger man thereafter, and for us around him, an even stronger Family. This accident did not take his life (or his legs in the end), but changed our lives as a Family forever. He became my role model for **resilience**! My drop dead gorgeous, well-educated and refined Mother, who wished to have six children, became his all-time Super Hero sidekick. WHAT A POWER COUPLE! I still thank them to this day, for teaching me to be resilient and kick adversity in the butt.

I grew up in Argentina and went to a prestigious all-girls British school, where in high school I learned that girls who are bullies are not to be feared. After a couple of years of putting up with glue in my hair, gum on my uniform, name calling and some major disruption to what I thought had been friendship for years before that, I realized that it was not what they were doing to me that mattered, but how I reacted to it. I made up my mind that they were lost and would find themselves eventually, one day. I stopped being afraid.

In early December 2001, while sitting in my backyard with my Father. He finally broke the silence and asked: "are you sure you want to do this?" My heart was accelerated and with confidence I replied: "no, but there is something inside of me that tells me I have to". A few weeks later, I left Buenos Aires, to embark on a journey I would have never imagined. Loaded with courage and determination, I hugged everyone tightly and moved to the United States of America. It was, at the time, the scariest thing I had ever done. Little did I know... I was only 22.

Before leaving my Family, Friends and a wonderful culture behind, my Mother told me that when I was little, I wanted to be "the star on the top of the Christmas tree". Just like that, she pushed me to conquer MY world by inspiring others. In MY world, I was about to do just that!

Interestingly enough, distance makes all fears seem small. Fast forward 20 years and I was able to create a home with a supporting, ridiculously handsome and loving Husband, three smart and inquisitive children and a successful business that allows me to inspire, but most importantly, BE inspired daily.

A few years into the making, I was "blessed" with experiencing a nasty divorce and becoming a single Mother, fighting an absurd custody battle, all while managing an entire division in-charge of over 2,000 employees. If this was not enough and to top it off, my boss was a womanizer bully asshole... WAIT!!! Did I just say that? Please do excuse my French! Allow me to rephrase that. My boss was an intolerable, habitually intimidation seeker, who thought himself to be Napoleon Bonaparte, and had a fascination for young Women. Now, why did I start off by saying I was blessed? Because, as the title of this chapter calls for, I do not believe in loosing nor do I believe in failure. I BELIEVE IN LEARNING! In retrospect, these experiences taught me that I am stronger than I think I am.

Looking back and making this recount, one day I asked myself: "seriously life, can I catch a break now?". Life then responded in a witty Fairy Godmother type of voice: *"oh no my dear, there is so much more for you to learn. Since you've asked, here is some additional training for you in this intricate recipe as follows:*

- *1 gallon of moving across the world, once again*

- *2 quarts of fathoming the move was a mistake (not to worry my dear, you will see this as an opportunity... eventually)*

- *1 pint of becoming the first female Vice President of the organization you work for, managing the most revenue generating and profitable region, while being the most underpaid Leader in the company (Congratulations! You will really enjoy this one.)*

- *1 ½ cups of an unmeasurable desire to expand your Family and 5 faulty attempts (but don't put too much thought into this one my dear, you are a ninja warrior and will not give up without a fight!)"*

These are stories I will elaborate on, next time we meet again (stay tuned). For now, and while you read this, as opposed to those TV talent shows I was telling you about at the beginning, I do not want you focused on the stories. Instead, I invite you to put on your own superhero outfit, hold my hand tight and jump with me into a rabbit hole that will lead us to my little toolbox. Let's search for those instruments I believe led me to becoming an unstoppable Woman. From here on, you get to pick which tools you take with you. Deal?

Here is the first:

Dream BIG, work HARD and MAKE IT HAPPEN! How about that for an opening statement?

⚒ **Adaptability**. Darwin once said that it is not the strongest or the most intelligent that survive but the most adaptable to change. I am here to tell you that change is the only constant in life. If you are able to gracefully embrace change, you will develop into a better leader of your life. Adaptability refers to our ability to be resourceful, to being able to adjust to whatever life throws at us, our ability to respond to change and Change is THE absolute catalyst for growth.

⚒ **Self-discipline**. With self-discipline anything is possible. I am all about possible, I work my tail off and stay focused. I create consistency through discipline. Ask yourself what you want most, not what you want now. You are solely responsible for everything that happens in your life, craft it! It belongs to you. You are the only one who can take YOU, to where YOU want to be. You can always use a Coach as a resource.

Belief and Conviction. Believing and having conviction in something or someone is an attitude. It takes time to develop, but it is well worth the work. Trust me! When you become convinced of your belief, is when magic starts to happen. I live by this rule. Believe in something hard enough where you become convinced it will happen. No need to know how or when, just that the Universe, God almighty or whomever that force is that you trust, will make it all work out.

Invest in knowledge. One should NEVER stop learning. Take that course, sign up for that webinar, participate in that conference, work on that certification, read, read, read... You will always find one million and ten excuses as to why you do not have time for any of this. What you may not be realizing is that the more you invest in your own knowledge, the more you grow and become unstoppable, because knowledge IS power!

Practice gratitude. The more I have practiced gratitude throughout my life, the more I have had to be grateful for. Believe it or not. It is the famous secret. Gratitude encompasses pretty much everything in your life. You can be grateful for what you have and get more of it, whether it is material, emotional or spiritual. Gratitude is one of the healthiest of human's emotions there are, it fills your heart with joy and you start radiating light like a sunshine, without even knowing it.

No dwelling allowed. During rough times, do not dwell on something for days. That will only deviate your focus from achieving your goals. Hear me out clearly, dwelling is an energy that takes you nowhere and accomplishes nothing. Dwelling in the past prevents you from doing something in the present. As a rule of thumb, I allow a stormy cloud over my head a few hours, no longer than 24. Once that period is over, the sun is shining and THE-SHOW-MUST-GO-ON.

All you need, is to transform your energy and put it in the right place, to continue to dream big, work your butt off and shoot for the stars. Once your head is in the right place, MAKE IT HAPPEN!

⚒ **Build your Tribe.** Behind every successful Woman there should be a tribe of other successful Women. You hear that? Not all Women are there to compete with you, that is such a prehistoric concept. Your tribe will cheer you on, will steer you in the right direction when you get off track, slap you several times in the face, if there is a need to bring you back to your senses, when your archenemy "the imposter syndrome" kicks in. THEY are the ones you can be vulnerable with because there is no judgmental thinking. THEY are the ones who will drop your name in a room filled with opportunities, just so that YOU can shine. THEY are the ones who keep you grounded and preserve your sanity in check. Why? Because THEY GET YOU! and you equally get them.

I cherish my Tribe, every single member of it. To you Ladies, because you all have something particularly special to offer to me as the Leader of my life, THANK YOU (you know who you are).

⚒ **Work-life balance...** say what? Stop chasing something that does not exist. In turn, find your happy medium. Hear me out, there is no such thing as work-life balance. There are work-life choices paired up with decisions. It is up to you to think wisely and have your priorities in check at all times, so that you can make the right decisions.

⚒ **Know your purpose** and work ravenously for your "why". Determine what drives you to wake up every morning and conquer the world. It could be your kids, your Family, your desire to be better, your commitment to someone you love, a Teacher who did not believe in you growing up or a boyfriend who put you down. Whatever it is that moves you, the same flame that fires up your heart, you must discover it! Remind yourself every day of what that is.

✂ **Respect who you are and embrace it**. As an introvert, I learned that it is ok to feel overwhelmed while in a public function. With this said, I now give myself a "time out", when I realize I have reached my cap of interactions. I elegantly throw a ninja smoke bomb and disappear, take a minimum of 30 minutes to put my energy in check and recharge. Being a foreigner, I also display a heavy accent which has been a burden for me for years. Not too long, I learned to be in peace with it and embrace the fact that I am different. I may speak with an accent but I do not think with one. Be in peace with yourself, at the end of the day and in your quiet thoughts, it is the only person you have to report to. Respect yourself for who you are and equally demand respect.

✂ **Will power over intelligence**. Why should will power triumph over IQ? You can have the highest IQ in the world, but without will power, you will accomplish nothing. You see, will power gives you the ability to control the urge to do what you want to do and resist short-term fulfilment, and instead, do what you must do, in the quest of long-term goals. Determination is what is going to take you to succeed in conquering your dreams.

✂ **Silence**. There is magic in silence. When in silence, we allow ourselves to listen, to hear, to think, to analyze, to understand, so that then we can purposely act. We live a life jam-packed with noise, literally. Around us, in social media, in gossip, in volunteered advise, and the list goes on. Make time to be in silence because silence is not empty, silence is actually filled with the answers you are seeking.

✂ **Personal Mantra**. Come up with a personal mantra that speaks to you. An affirmation to inspire you and motivate you to be the best version of yourself, day in and day out. Repeat it to yourself every time you need to hear it. Say it out loud. Convince yourself! I have a couple myself: "I choose courage over comfort" and "We can do this! We can do this! We can do this!". This last one, I use a lot around my kids too. I also share one with one of my dear Friends, which is "Make it happen!".

This book is filled with precious stories about being the best Leader of your life. I'm here to remind you that doubt kills more dreams than failure ever will. So, take a leap of faith, squash doubt with your best upper-cut and choose to WIN or LEARN!

My main mission in life is to inspire others to grow and during this journey so far, I have had the opportunity to touch many lives but it is those who touched mine, whether in a positive or negative way, who pushed me to make the decision that during this life there are only two options for me, to WIN or LEARN.

Yours truly,
Michèle, a Ninja Warrior at heart.

Karen Van Buren

Karen Jean the Beauty Queen

https://www.linkedin.com/in/karen-van-buren-b21573111

https://www.instagram.com/karenjeanthebeautyqueen

https://www.facebook.com/1beauty1queen

https://www.facebook.com/livingoutloud4life

https://www.facebook.com/livingoutloud4life2

Karen Jean the Beauty Queen; a name given by her parents at birth. Little did they know she would later be successful in the beauty industry. An Esthetician who has traveled on Regional and National Make Up Artist teams and freelanced as a beauty editor. She has planned and facilitated many women's events. She has been a guest speaker, keynote speaker and peer counselor with a concentration on women's issues. Her motivational speeches have empowered many. She has worked in ministry, counseled rape and domestic violence survivors, worked with the elderly and children fulfilling her life purpose in all these avenues. She is an activist; as well as an advocate of change. Her advocacy work has taken her to speak on Capitol Hill and be involved with amending bills. She is a cancer survivor that believes in "living out loud" and encourages woman that beauty comes from the inside. Her favorite place is with her family. She is a wife, mother, grandmother and "Momma K" or" Aunt Karen" to many!

Warpaint and Ribbons

By Karen Van Buren

To be 32 years old with a multitude of goals on my agenda, cancer was something that didn't fit into my script. I had a very busy and full life to live. I was raising my eight-year-old son as a single mother due to his father's incarceration and this little boy needed me now! I had just closed on a new house I had built, I was getting a business off the ground and had planned on starting a second business after that. I had a savings account and a plan. I wanted to start my fitness business for preschoolers. I loved fitness and working with children was my plan! Yes! A fitness business. I worked out 5-6 days a week, ate healthy, and took vitamins. I thought for a minute. How could I possibly have cancer when I was so health conscious? I planned to start a non-profit business to empower women after my fitness business was established. Life doesn't always go as planned, you know, but cancer though? Not cancer.

With buying a new house less than 2 years prior, having my son, an energetic dog, a successful career and a boyfriend in the NFL, cancer just didn't fit in. I was in charge of every activity my son participated in and I couldn't give that up! I couldn't get sick! We had meetings, an agenda and a sports centered life! I was Tiger Cub coach on Mondays while my son moved up the ranks in Boy Scouts. I was an assistant teacher for the children's choir on Wednesdays at our church, which was a mega church with close to 8,000 members. We were living in Charlotte, North Carolina at the time and the Carolina Panthers had a star player who attended our church. He was my eight year old's favorite player and an extra motivation that made him want to go to church. My son met him at church during my cancer journey. Thank you Steve Smith for making a scary time in my son's life a lot better. Later that season Steve helped carry our Panthers to the Superbowl and although we didn't win, my son's world was brighter as his mother fought for her life.

Sports were my son's focus aside from schoolwork. We alternated what sport he did depending on the time of year. Sports were filled in with other activities on alternating days. This kid did football, basketball, baseball, soccer and rugby. We juggled sports, Boy Scouts, chess club, Odyssey of the Mind, Karate and Taekwondo. He attended a project-based gifted school where he served on student council and carried the weight of at least 3 hours of homework each evening. I was room parent at his school, heading up all the classroom parties and activities while doing outreach to parents. I would solicit parent volunteers, but I loved spearheading the parties so much that I always had a theme and even matching colored foods for the seasonal parties. Talk about OCD, I have to laugh at myself reflecting on that time now. I was Team Parent for all the sports organizing snack and drink lists, giving handouts to parents or direction when questioned. I was one of the main parent helpers at Karate and Taekwondo as well and trained the children with a teacher for Odyssey of the Mind. So you see, I didn't have time for cancer. My schedule was structured and full, and definitely could not fit in cancer.

I had just stopped working full time to start my business, so I was treating it like a full-time job. I had people to meet each day to network with, working to land accounts while doing presentations numerous times. So many people liked my idea, that I started interviewing people to be possible subcontractors. I could only be in one place at a time to conduct a class. This all came flooding into my head as I heard the doctor say cancer. I needed to get to the point. What did I need to do to get rid of it and get back to my life? This was the ultimate intrusion while interrupting my plans. Little did I know at this point that it would be as if someone pulled the carpet out from underneath me! My schedule would be interrupted, my energy would be zapped, my limp body would be on a cold floor in the bathroom after throwing up repeatedly and I would experience some agonizing side effects from treatment that made a wheelchair my means of transportation.

Wait! The doctor was explaining it looked to be "a cancer" with the probability of surgery, chemotherapy and radiation. He explained in a very matter-of-fact way that I was extremely young to be receiving this diagnosis. My tumor was large, so my treatment plan had to be more aggressive. I asked immediately how he was sure it was "a cancer" without a biopsy. This question piggy backed him informing me that they would schedule a biopsy to confirm this suspicious tumor. His answer was simply... "If it walks like a duck, quacks like a duck, it is a duck." After my appointment, I still remember my father, who I affectionately call my "Papa Bear," calling that doctor a quack when we spoke. He said "Quack like a duck... he's a quack! Just wait until you get the biopsy. He doesn't know what he's talking about." Reflecting back now, my dad was probably trying to stay as positive as he could due to losing his father less than two months beforehand. My grandfather, too, had battled cancer in his last days of life, but ultimately died from complications of numerous health issues. Honestly, we all have our own way of dealing with stressors and my dad was remaining optimistic in my eyes. He couldn't accept his "little girl" may have to face cancer. Consequently, my mindset was hopeful as well. When I spoke to my mother, she appeared positive, too. Her voice never trembled. She concentrated on her history of benign cysts. We agreed in that moment I probably inherited the same trait. I'm sure my parents were not prepared for the calls they received from me, but I'm grateful for their upbeat attitudes and positivity! I was on the other end of the phone feeling like I could beat cancer if that was the card I was dealt. I wasn't scared or worried. My focus was on being proactive and getting the biopsy.

I decided to call my closest girlfriends. I knew they would react to my news based on my delivery, so I was careful in how I explained the possibility. Like roll call on the Mickey Mouse Club, I called each one. I was reminded of their same loving support I felt just three years earlier: the day I was stood up on my wedding day. I was humbled, distressed and devastated that day, but pushed through as I always have. As I reflected on that time, I remember how much my girlfriends helped me. There was no way cancer could defeat my fighting spirit. Reminding myself that no problem is insurmountable. Remembering everything in life is temporary, including emotion. I would not wear doom and gloom. It was not the woman I stood for. I believe your attitude is half the battle in life. Your perception of your situation coupled with your resourcefulness helps you survive. Past trials or tribulations bring to fruition one's true character. These are my directives I apply to my existence. I choose to concentrate on many pivotal blissful moments I've captured along the years with loved ones. I know tomorrow is not promised. I realize any hardships I've encountered have truly formed my "walk through the fire" persona.

My mortality was not something I had faced in terms of a disease, but I did identify with the feelings. I had instances that struck the same raw emotion. A gang rape at 15 years old marked the possibility of death at conclusion as it was happening. Luckily it didn't, but I temporarily died on the inside as I processed what was taken from me. Shortly after, I was date raped as well, but couldn't use rape again in my vocabulary. I felt like something was wrong with me. I carried my pain on the inside with no evidence on the outside. I struggled with depression as well as suicidal attempts. I ultimately ended up in a very toxic, domestic violence relationship in my early 20s. Again, I felt unsure of my own mortality as I navigated through this abusive relationship over three-and-a-half long years.

I went for the biopsy. I have no recollection of fear. A couple days later I received the news. I remember sitting at home in my office. I was documenting my experience when the call came. I was very gracious on my end of the phone, but I immediately felt anger. A surge of energy came from within. A powerful energy that felt like a warrior going into battle. I was ready to fight! My own spiritual belief told me the "enemy" was attacking me. I had to claim what was going to happen! I remember standing up from my computer saying "Lucifer, I know you're lurking. You have no power over me or my body right now. You will get out of my life, my body and my house right now!" I was loud and passionate as I said it... as I was speaking, I was walking through my house. I opened my front door, elevating my voice even louder as I spiritually kicked the devil out of my house that day!

It was June of 2003 and just a month prior I was told I had the start of colon cancer. No treatment was needed since they were precancerous lesions. They were cut out and the pathology revealed the margins were clear. Now hearing I had an aggressive tumor in my left breast, I needed to understand it all. The pathology report confirmed two types of breast cancer as well as it being hormone receptive. In simple terms, my hormones were feeding my breast cancer. Eventually I was told I would die in two years and be lucky if I made it to five. I know my faith and sense of humor sustained me through this period of my life. I woke up each day with a warrior mentality and gained my survivor skills through each experience I endured. There was a constant reminder with the cancer that I was in a battle... a battle for my life. So as I would wake up each day, I would go to the mirror to put my "WARPAINT" on for my new "pink ribbon cause" I was fighting. This was war and I was in the fight of my life.

I did a series of surgeries over the next couple years. I got poked with needles galore. Living with a disease I couldn't feel, but yet when treatment began I experienced pain. I thought medicine made you feel better, but with chemotherapy, that's not the case. There is a war going on in your body. The chemo agents are designed to kill the tumor. These tumors are nothing but mutated cells in our bodies. So while the chemo is trying to kill the bad cells it is also killing good cells... much like WAR! There are side effects with any drug. I fought through each one. I suffered a drug-induced brain injury as a result of the anti-nausea medication given to me during chemotherapy. I spent over three years stuck in spasms! My chin locked on my right shoulder, never giving me a break. I had constant, excruciating pain. My spasms moved to my legs, making it impossible to walk. For short durations each time, I was forced to use a wheelchair. Homebound most of this time, I was unable to drive since I couldn't move my head. During radiation therapy, I was told my skin would break down. I slowly figured out that statement meant my flesh was being burned. Eventually the burning caused me to see raw flesh.. OUCH!!!

My patience was being tested and my strength stretched beyond my mental comprehension. In these moments, it was apparent how important my health was to me and how much I had taken for granted in my life prior to this. My new "warpaint and ribbons" mentality was crystal clear. I was immersed in a battle while having a cause I was fighting for! My faith saved me! Every single day I spiritually put my warpaint on as I fought my pink ribbon disease. To think about faith, one must abandon logic and reason. Logic involves facts, while reason is broader because it's based on truth. Faith is a belief so strong that no person or circumstance can alter the outcome. When armed with faith in battle, there is no ammunition that can penetrate or destroy the subject at hand. First you must believe in what you are fighting for as well as never give power to resistance. Your mind must be completely in control of your emotions while faith intercedes the battle at hand.

Not only riddled with cancer amidst this battle, but now I had doctors saying my brain injury was permanent. My head was flopping like a fish out of water when experiencing the spasms in my neck. Eventually, my head locked as this neurological disorder continued. Another trial I endured was conceiving a baby after being told chemotherapy caused my infertility. My ex-husband and I were discouraged as the medical team of doctors encouraged us to abort the baby due to possible complications based on medical research. We were told we would lose the baby or it would have major malformations since the baby was conceived during chemotherapy treatment. Against all odds, I went to term with this pregnancy. We had a very healthy baby boy! It was through this circumstance that I reaffirmed my faith. I prayed constantly. I trusted God with my health along with the baby I was having. Again, my faith was my rock.

Given two to five years to live, I learned to navigate through trusting the process. An unending, unquestionable and unwavering faith did not allow fear or doubt to cloud my thought process. Peace was a forever presence I carried with me. I adapted these attributes into my daily existence. My choice that required discipline. I started to look at cancer like getting a flat tire. There are a couple options when one gets a flat tire, but it's key to not panic and remember it's only temporary. No state of being or any occurrence is ever permanent. Grasping this knowledge is powerful for your soul; it will cause your spirit within to be unstoppable. It was then, and after eighteen years of survival that I embraced being an unstoppable woman.

Lisa Vasquez

Founder Of All About Women Inc

https://www.linkdin.com/in/lisa-vasquez-7883b5218

www.instagram.com/lisa.m.vasquez

Lisa Vasquez is a registered radiologic technologist who has specialized in breast health mammography imaging for the past 40 years. Lisa Vasquez has a passion for uncovering menopause weight gain, gut health and metabolic resistance, a visionary for the future of self-care. After working 40 years in radiology studying the body's internal connection through a radiographic lens. Lisa has integrated a certification as a holistic health coach to better serve women in their post-reproductive series of life self-care. Life is a craft getting to the real root cause of why the body is malfunctioning and correcting those root causes, to reclaim and be BOSS of their own bodies.

Lisa is the founder of All About Women Inc. with a passion-driven purpose to enhance the ability she has established in forty years. She continues to grow in the field of health coaching while integrating a new movement with a full understanding of the internal body functions through the lens of a radiology camera. She now links the human anatomy internal study into an effective educational coaching program, creating a holistic health makeover coaching in mind, body, and spirit.

While she is out living life, she enjoys family life with her husband and canine kids, outdoors entertainment, and just lazy days enjoying nature.

If I Do Not Go Within: I Go Without

By Lisa Vasquez

I grew up on Chicago southside in a Hispanic culture middle class family, the youngest of four siblings. With great gratitude I thank my mother and father for providing me a balanced life with a strong understanding of working to be a productive citizen. I attended Holy Cross Catholic school, their mission is nurturing the entire person in mind body and spirit all necessities for a happy healthy balanced life. This opportunity was a gift in my basket of knowledge, to explore the soulish realm learning the language of living in the light verse's darkness. So, life began to develop as a unique individual filling my basket of life up with all new tools of opportunities that we can all pick up along the way.

The" gift is in the basket" we all start at zero to begin the race of life and every decade brings a new start all over. It's never too late to start filling your basket of life up with new tools of opportunities that will update you along the way. The" gifts in the basket" will also come with dark shadows. Here is where you meet resistance, important for character-building these tools will be essential. We all have a choice what to fill our baskets with to keep us fueled for the journey of life's intersection and different seasons of life. Harvest time, drought seasons, there are different cycles in life. Some people get stuck in the fall season and never see what could spring up later.

Some great steppingstones, you pick up on the road. It adds to the beauty of living with an education that can create a change. For me this was an invaluable opportunity that my parents gave me. The ability to explore my passion and strengthen myself as I come to know God. I believe in my journey of understanding how to cultivate the entire person, by engaging in the human need for physical, mental, social and spiritual nourishment. It all started when the seed was planted, as I developed this structure in the 60's that led to the foundation and framework of my life's purpose today. Empowering women across the continuum of selfcare awareness.

Today 41 years as a Registered Radiology/Mammographer professional imager I studied the inside city of life. Radiology is used to diagnose or treat patients by recording images of the internal structure of the body to assess the presence or absence of disease, foreign objects and structural damage or irregularity. Back in September,1981 I did work in radiology, I was a portable technologist. I called myself the hospital photographer and I went to patient rooms to care for them in a more convenient way. During this adventure I was able to visit every department that was in the house.

From the Newborn nursery, intensive care units, recovery room, surgery, psychiatric units, all the way down to the morgue. You live with death walking the halls and life entering into the world. My benefit of all this was the education each nursing station provided me with. Any questions I would have on this journey it helped me build the framework which helped me create my purpose for life. Outside the medical world we generally only see superficial, the outside cover of the body the external. Growing up in the medical world I had such a good understanding of body functions from inside.

I wanted to learn more of our bodies internal communication, to develop a deeper inner connection. In January 2018 I graduated and became a Certified Integrative Nutrition Holistic Health coach to study about how to create a behavioral change with mind, body and soul. I am in pursuit of working with women. My mission is to ultimately encourage motivation by presenting women with an attitude for survival, retooling women to use their power within. This will ensure the best possible care and satisfaction of understanding the rhythm to empower their own body.

How all this started was the dream of a 15 year old Latina, my first conversation with God. It was 1976 when I went within to call upon the power of GOD. It was to sustain me and keep me safe as I must now walk through the valley of darkness. What I knew for sure was I was coming to a turning point, things were happening in the neighborhood. Young pregnancies were occurring, drinking, drugs were being introduced into the neighborhood. I was in a relationship young and I was sure this was what I did not want for my future. So I went within to check with my creator.

The unfolding of my story of life had already been written and to communicate above as well as below according to His will, I made a request. Life was becoming challenging so my 'Big ASK" was for the next five years I prayed asking him could He bring me out of this so I could go to X ray school at age 18 and could I be out of this relationship by age 21. I prayed that this all could be done for me to my father, ACCORDING TO THY WILL. I prayed saying "I WILL give my whole life to you and I would never ask questions anymore and my path would be your path. Everything that you would want I would learn to know. I would be there according to thy will be done." PLEASE help me Lord. At that moment a choice was being made. A test of my human spirit connecting, to communicate with my higher power. My first life seed was being planted, to grow my tree of hope. I am 15 years old and a five-year goal was planted to create a path. To lead me I had a vision and I made a choice to change my life, everything about it.

At the time, there was a lot of opposition. I had been taught to look deeper in self for the truth in which you are living. Darkness is clever and from my view this was a dark shadow. Like a blanket blocking a view on the surface but when you look within you find there are opportunities covered underneath what you do not see. I wanted to make sure I would not go without, if I stay connected within.

While I was out living life in the light and with darkness, I was accepted into the SCHOOL OF RADIOLOGY TECHNOLOGY. It was a Saint Joseph hospital based program, designed with theory and hands on experience. I had arrived given the key to venture away and expand my horizons in Healthcare.

The beauty in this and how I know God sees me was because 18 years prior I was born here. To be welcomed back and given a bonus to my life could only be part of the divine plan that has been written. I was not savvy in how to enroll for a program. Generally you should apply to many schools, I only applied to this one and I was accepted on the spot. There is no need to wait for the happy invitation you receive when you are accepted into a program. With that being said, four decades later and many conversations waiting on God, I journaled my life writing love letters to my Heavenly Father. Especially for my birthday caviar dreams and champagne wishes.

I had goals every five years up to age thirty. The roads were long. When you start your journey with your soul, you arrive at different intersections of life. It is all a part of the journey to meet the MOTHERSHIP. You will sail through storms of life, we all have our beast of burdens. For me it was with siblings, abuse, emotional and homelessness. When you are surrounded by crowds but yet always feeling alone, passing through the toxic wasteland, and indulging in toxic substances to feel no pain, pray your way out of this environment. When you are guided by your Higher self you know this shall all pass, you just need to survive the darkness to come in to living in the light. No one escapes the darkness, we all have to pass through it. Keep the lamp on your feet lit so you can see where you are going. Being cast out was a big one FOR ME until you learn you were never meant to fit in. You think you are supposed to fit in, when in reality ones road is created to standout.

As I developed in my career my specialty all about women as a breast health advocate, we are now facing a more brutal body sabotage. In the past twenty years, I started to have different conversations with women. A lot of their health is declining compared to what women presented to me back in the eighties, when life had a healthier environment. No crap food, no fast meal, no loss of energy because there was no distraction from the electronics. Women have not slept for days, every shape and size of women living in the cycle of change, is in combat to survival.

Statistics show 50% of adults are diagnosed with chronic illness, 68% are overweight, 70% are on prescription drugs, 80% are mentally or emotionally not flourishing and 97.3 % are not maintaining healthy habits, decent nutrition, adequate exercise, smoking and healthy body composition. Here is why I integrated and became a certified HHC for a health make over, integrating education on nourishing mind body and soul. What is a health coach? health coaches consider all aspects of a person's life. We address a wide variety of wellness factors. We work in conjunction with physicians', nurses and dieticians and serve to fill a void in our current healthcare system. We serve as wellness mentors, we help people find that food is medicine, relationships, fitness routines and lifestyle that create a change to make you feel your best.

Today so many TV specials are showing us major transformation, exercise shows and weight loss shows. They take unknown people and make them a superstar. They take the worst cook and turn them into maybe OK cooks etc. We are very fascinated by stories of transformation because it shows what was and what can be right in front of our eyes. Imagine food, drinks and body in motion and sleep. These are the most basic requirements for life. We all have to eat and drink, keep the body moving to stay fresh and energized and sleep is so important for cellular repair. I call this the time when all your body mechanics come out. When the body is at rest to repair you and use the nourishment you provide it to sustain, you accept. With all the statistics I presented you, here is where we are creating more body sabotage.

The city of life has a lot of inside shops closed down because the nutrients are being replaced with crap food toxins and loss of sleep. You have now confused the brain by taking the body out of the sleep cycle. The five major things we need is air to live, water to drink, sleep for cellular repair, food to fuel and improve the quality. We have discovered we eat so much sugar, which can create a lot of mental changes. Because food is our mood, we are what we absorb. We fluctuate with different changes, we energize ourselves with sugar but with sugar we drop and when we drop we create the mood change. When we eat healthy with food as medicine, we find a balance. You begin to lose weight, we have no cravings, we've become smarter because brain fog has lifted, we become more energized, our skin appears healthier, and we become looking more ageless. This is why changing your food is necessary to change your mood.

When I began my journey to create a change, my first encounter of life out of balance came to me at 30 years old. I had just left the in 80s and was growing up in my twenties. That is when all the music stopped, partying stopped, the dancing stopped and do you remember stretchy straight leg pants that came out? everyone was wearing these so we eliminated wearing jeans with a buttons and zippers. We were all now wearing stretch pants so nobody is noticing the weight gain that was approaching. One day I went to try to get back into my jeans and realized they didn't fit. It was a very rude awakening for me, I started out in my 20s at a weight of 120. My highest would be 126.

Here it is 1988, as I mentioned in the beginning every ten years we have a new beginning, I am now 27 years old in preparation for my next adventure that is upcoming at age 30 so I stopped and I checked within. I prepared my birthday celebration to be in Las Vegas to celebrate my 27th year. I always traveled alone, all my friends had a different lifestyle to live so I couldn't wait on them. I'd have to travel alone if I wanted to go anywhere. I arrived in Las Vegas on Thursday, I figured being in Las Vegas it's hard to see that you are by yourself. You're in a crowd and nobody knows who you're with, so it was the best way and safest way to protect myself traveling alone. I spent the day having another conversation with God, setting up new dreams, new hopes, new champagne wishes for my future.

When you speak on these terms, you're always three days from nowhere because you never know what the plan is. All you could do is hope and dream that as above as well as below, that hopefully because the divine master's plan is already created.

As long as you live in the vision in your head, instead of competing with people on the outside of your world. My mission always took place from the mission. Inside the cycle and the timeline that I lived by was always programmed and written in the stars. The only challenge was to stay on track and hope that my preparation for the future would transform and match up with the vision. In 1990 I was getting ready and preparing to enter my new life adventure. At thirty years old, the fog had lifted and I found myself at 163 lbs, a story for another time because now time has passed. I am 46 years old 173 lbs and I could not even do a pushup at the time. I enrolled myself with a coach and to date I can say at age 58 I entered THE MRS. NEVADA-AMERICAN Pageant, Mrs. Southern Highlands weighing in at 130 lbs and Lady Las Vegas International 40+ Beauty pageant, Mrs. Chicago and today at age 60 I created a health makeover and enrolled myself in my program and am now living in my twenty year old body 124 LBS and by the way I look today you would never know what roads of fluctuation and battle scars really exist.

I am the results of: Internal Connections / HOLISTIC HEALTH MAKE OVER COACHING. https://www.thehealthydeviant.com/ statistics

The only way to change is to understand and realize THE SOULISH REALM

IN MY SOUL I HAVE SELF CONSCIOUS

IN MY SPIRIT I HAVE GOD CONSCIOUS

IN MY BODY I HAVE WORLD CONSCIOUS (T.D. JAKES AMERICAN AUTHOR)

Never doubt that a small group of thoughtful, committed citizens can't change the world, indeed, it's the only thing that ever has. (Margaret Mead)

Thank you to the she rises community for creating an unstoppable woman!!

Jami Bolduc

Author

www.instagram.com/jamideeboo

www.facebook.com/jami.dee.boo

I was born raised in the heart of Minnesota. I currently still reside here with the love of my life, Paul. I have no children of my own, but I have been blessed with many nieces and nephews. I am six out of seven children. Sadly, there is only four of us left. There has been a lot of loss in a short amount of time. Recently my mother. Grieving has taught me to embrace life more. I stay busy helping in my community, it gives me a sense of accomplishment and enrichment in my life. My greatest achievement has been receiving a patent from the United States Patent Office and I am currently pursuing bringing my product to market. Be fearless in the pursuit of what sets your soul on fire. Always remember, that no matter what you are going through in life, make each day count.

Infinitely Resilient

By Jami Bolduc

Growing up in a small town with my 5 sisters and 1 brother, I was forced to grow up sooner than most. My father struggled with alcoholism. My mother was diagnosed with cancer at a young age and that took a toll on her mental health as her physical health was compromised. She couldn't perform daily duties so my sister Penni was her caregiver most days. Those were some tough childhood years, but we were always loved and had what we needed. As we got older I found myself being treated unfairly, I moved out at a young age and I landed my first job at the age of 13. I quickly found myself helping raise a few nieces and nephews. Meanwhile, I was going to school maintaining my responsibilities that were expected of me. I found that these tasks were above and beyond of a girl that age, but we remained solid as a family though we were living apart.

My nieces and nephews are the little loves of my life. I was present when each one was born and that was something truly special to watch. I have a special bond with each one and they have made me so proud. I have the privilege of being a God mommy to most of them. My love for them is everlasting.

As time went on, I wanted something more in my life, something exciting but rewarding. I enrolled myself in college. My dream was to be a doctor. Unfortunately, it did not go as planned. My aunt was diagnosed with cancer and called on me to be her caregiver until she passed away. That's what lead me into healthcare. I knew then what my purpose was in this life and that was to give of myself, my time, love, compassion. It was challenging but very fulfilling.

Some of the best things happen unexpectedly and that is exactly what happened when I met my soulmate Paul. We had an instant connection and it truly was love at first sight. I was such a broken young woman I did not understand how or why he could fall in love with someone like me but I realized Paul was broken too. He was heavy into drinking and struggled with anger. He was stuck in an emotional messy middle of life and was in need of saving. I helped him through some dark times. Not only did he change his life for me but most importantly, He did for himself. I was his angel and he was my hero. Together we created a real love story that took years to build. It took sacrifices, mistakes, compromises, and forgiveness. I am proud of the life we share today. Paul makes me feel like I am a queen, He looks at me with the same love in his eyes like the first day we met. He continues to take me on dates and surprises me with little gifts and spontaneous road trips. This man is my rock and solitude and I am beyond excited for the day I call my Prince my husband.

Shortly after meeting Paul I was faced with my worst fear, I got a call my father, the man who I loved first, the man who believed in me, passed away suddenly. I was overwhelmed with so many emotions, so much so I ended up at the emergency department as I thought I was dying of a broken heart. I did not think I could go on. I was 24 years old without a father. I never got to say goodbye, I did not get one last hug, I did not get to tell him I love him one last time. Though my father struggled, He was a wonderful man and father. He was a gentle soul and loved by so many who knew him. I did not really understand death and grieving. I started having panic and anxiety attacks daily and my mental health was compromised. I started going to therapy to help me through the darkness I was carrying. In that decision I learned so much about me. It wasn't easy talking to a stranger about my life and digging up things from childhood but I learned that everything I was feeling was valid and it was perfectly normal to have hate, anger, sadness, and, abandonment feelings. When I was just a year old my live in uncle started to molest me and that went on for 7 years. I had never talked about it until I went to therapy. I needed to heal and move on and the first step was allowing myself to feel all the pain to be able to accept everything I was going through. I walked away feeling like a much stronger woman when I found my own strength and courage.

Shortly after my father passed away, my mother suffered several massive heart attacks and a whole new journey started. She spent several weeks in the hospital and my siblings and I stayed by her side night and day. I was terrified that I would lose my mother, as she laid there on life support I prayed to God that he would wrap his healing arms around my mother and heal her, to please let her wake up. Day after day of the same thing, I decided to go to the hospital chapel and get on my knees and continue to lean into God and beg for a miracle, to please hear and answer. Several days later my mother woke up on her birthday, The doctors came to me and said "your mother is alive today due to higher power" I can't explain the pure joy, relief, and eternal gratefulness my heart felt. We were able to bring my mother home once she was in stable condition and take care of her daily needs where she was most comfortable. It did not take her long to get back in the kitchen cooking and baking, making all her children's favorite goodies. It was a wonderful sight to see her doing everything she loved doing again. My mother made each and every day count.

From 2004 to 2021 a father, mother, and 3 sister's left this earth. Dealing with each loss brought different emotions. Never in my life have I felt so alone. The stress and depression made me physically sick. I had a severe panic attack the afternoon my mom passed away and I went to the emergency department, I was met by Dr. Lance Fisher, I will never forget how he helped me, he handled me with such kindness, compassion, and understanding. He prayed with me and just simply listened and let me cry on him. He did offer some words of encouragement and I listened to them. As I was laying there, I looked at the doctor and I said, "I got to get out of here, I should not be here. My mom would be so disappointed in me for showing weakness. I am stronger than this and I have a funeral to plan". Dr. Fisher said "You can stay here as long as you need to, I am here for you". I don't think he will ever know how grateful I am to him when I was so vulnerable and at rock bottom. When everything sank in I was hit with so much darkness and sadness. Every day was doom. I had to find beneficial ways to get through this. I started writing, it was a great way to release my thoughts. I surrounded myself with people who I could express my feelings to. I cried for days and I would question why. I wanted understanding to all the suffering. As I sat in so much darkness and sorrow there was no escape. I had to allow myself to feel every emotion in order to accept their deaths. It was my new reality. My mother and I shared a bond that most will never understand. She was truly one of a kind and the one person who accepted me for me and her love was pure and unconditional. She was an amazing woman and guided me with the very best advice. She really did always know best. My heart knew no greater heartache.

I really needed the 3 siblings I have left but unfortunately we aren't as solid anymore.

The closeness we once shared is no longer. Everyone grieves differently, and pain changes us. We all grew apart and that seemed like worthy of grieving in itself, I prayed hard for more togetherness, more love, and more understanding of one another. I will hang onto hope that we will one day have what we had. Our mother taught us that love trumps all, that's the way to peace.

When I look at back at everything I went through, I see pain, heartache, mistakes, and, regrets. When I look into my future I see, pride in myself, strength, and, new beginnings. I am only choosing to move forward from now on to a better and brighter future. When I wake up every morning I thank God for another blessed day. When

I go to bed every night I thank God for giving me the ability to accomplish great things.

Having weathered some of life's biggest storms I am here to talk about it all, even when it would have been easier to throw in the towel. All of this has made me unstoppable. I took all my brokenness and turned it into power and force. My ability to conquer any challenge is resilience. I strive to be a better version of myself each day and remember I am enough.

I will continue to live to help others and one way is to give back to my community where I am needed. Thanksgiving, I love to fill baskets full of food and give them away to families who are less fortunate. Christmas, I love to donate to those who have fallen on hard times. I also donate to the local women's center, Teen challenge, multiple group homes, and hospital patients. For me, there is no better feeling than bringing peace and joy to others.

I have made some lifelong friendships not only through my annual paying it forward, but through my hard times. These friends have been there for me when I was having a hard time seeing the light, sat with me through the nights when having anxiety attacks or just couldn't sleep. We have shared many of our trials and tribulations and have given each other advice or sometimes just a listening ear with a hug when no words need to be spoken. However, my favorite times are the girl's weekends, out of town shopping trips, going out for lunch and just hanging out with my friends, drinking cold coffee or Mello Yellow, laughing, talking and just enjoying life. Some of my friends are my biggest supporters I have. Some days I could not make it without these friends of mine, I hold each and every one of them close to my heart.

I am also working on something very exciting, a few years ago I was granted a patent on a brand-new women's product that I can't wait for an opportunity to bring to market. It was a dream come true to get a patent on something I designed and created. I worked tirelessly on making the product a reality. It would be even a bigger dream to see on the shelves someday. Along this inventing journey I met some really wonderful people, they gave me knowledge, advice, and encouragement to keep moving, but I also met some not so good ones. I was too trusting and got taken advantage of which delayed my process. I will continue to move on to better opportunities. Hopefully someday I can share with all the world.

In addition to my current life events I am planning to tackle the opiate crisis in this country. It is an epidemic and having lost 3 sisters in their 40's due to addiction to these types of drugs was devastating. It will not be easy, but neither was going through their loss. I'm sure they all didn't expect to pay the ultimate price. We have 7 children without mothers. They all helplessly watched their mothers fight demons no one could ever understand. I will fight for Jodi, Misti, and Kristi. I will make sure to fulfil my promise to my sisters that Nathan, Hailee, Jacob, GeNae, Wesley, Audianna, and Nicholas are always taken care of and loved with every fiber of my being.

My purpose for sharing my story with all of you is to show that you too can be unstoppable. Every story is significant and valuable. There is no shame in sharing and possibly helping someone who might be going through similar situations. Writing all this was healing for me. This just might help someone who is suffering heal. I am not a victim for sharing my story, I am a warrior setting the world on fire with truth, transparency, and reality. I challenge you to step out of your comfort zone and use your incredible potential that you carry within you to let your guard down and use your talents, gifts and creativity that were naturally given to you. Live life like no tomorrow.

Leslie Gaudet

Mindset and Emotional Awareness Coach

https://www.linkedin.com/in/leslie-gaudet-744713113

https://www.instagram.com/lesligaudet

https://www.facebook.com/lgaudet55

https://lesliegaudetcoaching.podia.com

Leslie is a Mindset and Emotional Awareness Coach for women. She helps her clients achieve self-awareness around their emotional triggers through shifting their mindset so that they can make better decisions when they respond, which allows them to bring more balance, peace, and harmony into their life.

Her coaching certifications include Group Coaching, Emotional Intelligence, and most recently Spiritual Life Coach.

She works closely with her clients starting with mindset because that is the foundational piece to self-love and self-acceptance. She teaches her clients about triggers, how to spot and understand their own, so that they can become more self-aware of their trigger moments and emotional responses.

With proven tools and techniques, and with her guidance, her clients tap into and discover their true potential to living their life and loving the life they are living.

Leslie believes that when you Change Your Brain, You will Transform Your Life.

Time: How Taking It Back Save My Life

By Leslie Gaudet

I always knew it was possible to change careers, or rather, to live a life you love doing what you love. The evidence was there because the world was changing, and women were not only forging their own paths, but they were encouraging and supporting one another along the way.

I knew it was possible for me too. The evidence was right in front of me, but I was hesitant for two reasons. First, because I was really good at what I did and second because I was really good at what I did and I thought that maybe you only get to be good at one thing, especially people like me, and that I should count my blessings.

When I say people like me, I mean people who grew up poor as dirt, living in social housing, feeling like an outsider and unworthy of more. There were three strikes against me. One, I was poor. Two, I was a different color than my mom. Three, my father wasn't in the picture and so, we did not fit into what society deemed worthy or deserving of a second look or of success or of leading a better life (or at least, that's what I told myself).

You see, I grew up in a single parent home with a white mother and two younger brothers who also looked like me but they were lighter than I because we didn't share the same blood father. Their father, my stepfather, gave me his name when he married my mom, but that union didn't last long unfortunately.

My mom and my dad (whom I will only refer to as my birth father) never married. He didn't come into the picture as owning that he was my father until I was 14 years old and he came in hard. Only then did he want me because he tried to convince me into

119

going to live with him and his new wife and family thinking that I would be better off living with him and that somehow he was a much better choice than the woman I had been calling mom (and who also filled the shoes of my father because he wasn't around).

I think that this is where my first experience around rejection started; when I realized that my father didn't want me until it suited him to take me away from the only parent I knew and who was fierce in her love and support for me. He tried to turn me against her, but it didn't work.

The sad thing is, the only thing that that did for our relationship (his and mine) was fracture it beyond repair (for me at that time) and it only solidified the one with my mom because she was a strong woman who took care of her babies and never gave up on us just because it was hard and she often had to work extra hard just so that her kids wouldn't go without. This is where I got my resilience and strength from. My mom gave me so much and I will tell you why in just a bit but let me lean into my story just a little bit more, my why for change, the reason that time was so important, and how taking it back saved my life.

Just before I turned 20, I started a career in law as a Legal Assistant and I loved the fast-paced energy and the money of course. I loved the hustle and grind and was always finding ways to move up and better my craft because I wanted to make more money and the only way to do that was to get better and better and that also meant trading time for money because I was working hard and a lot. You see, when you are young, the chase doesn't phase you, or at least it didn't for me until it finally did but we will get to that in just a bit.

Fast forward a few decades, at 45 years of age, and deep into my career of choice, I was starting to feel the burnout and I started thinking that there has to be more to life, but I couldn't quite figure out what that better life looked like or better yet, what I possibly might be deserving enough to step into. My emotions started to turn extremely sour and ugly. I didn't like the woman I was becoming. I was blaming everything and everyone around me for my "lot" in life. I was mad at my husband because I thought it was his job to make me happy and I was resentful because he didn't seem to have the same types of work pressures that I did and so I was always mad at him. I didn't like the life I was living. In fact, I could go so far as to state "I hated my life at the time". I know that hate is such a powerful word, but I want to be truthful with you so that you have a deeper understanding for what I am about to tell you.

You see, I've been a Legal Assistant/Paralegal for almost 4 decades and for the last 3 years, I've been a Life Coach for women and more recently a Mindset and Emotional Awareness Coach for women where I have been teaching them how little mindset shifts can empower them to lean into living their lives with more joy, gratitude and love, but my journey to becoming a Life Coach was not on my radar at first. In fact, self-love was on my radar because as I told you earlier, I didn't like the life I was living, and I blamed everyone and everything around me for the life I was living that I truly hated.

Little did I know that I could make change but I allowed almost another 10 years pass me by and by then I was not only feeling the emotional burden but my body soon followed and at almost 55 years young, I started to feel "not quite myself". I became very concerned that if I didn't make changes in my life, that I would possibly die from a heart attack and that is when it became real for me that change was not only a wish but something that was a must.

I was stressed to the max and the little time that I had left for myself, which wasn't much, was spent sitting in front of the television eating dinner, watching sitcoms and feeling lonely. Lonely because the time that we had for each other, my husband and myself, wasn't really quality time listening and connecting with one another and that was putting me into a deep depression.

I didn't know how to express how I was feeling without it coming across as demanding more time or blaming that the time spent wasn't good enough and that was putting a strain on our marriage.

On top of that, I was feeling extremely overwhelmed at work, putting in long hours, commuting a long way to work and back home every day, and even bringing work home with me on the weekends, and so that started cutting into the little time that I did have for anything other than work.

I wasn't feeling well. My body was starting to physically manifest how I was feeling because I couldn't sleep, I wasn't eating healthy nor hydrating well, and I started feeling like something in my body was "off".

It all came to a head one day when I finally hit my "enough" moment and I soon realized that if I didn't finally start taking responsibility for myself and start looking at what was possible for me, that there were only two options. I was either going to keep living a life I truly despised and have a heart attack and die OR I was going to have to get into the game of life (my game of my life) so that I could find purpose for myself and so I chose me. I finally started looking for ways to make change in my life that would help me to like myself again and to start living my life, and that was the first step to taking back my time.

When my husband and I decided to make some changes that would lead to living a more fulfilled and joyful life, and ultimately strengthen our marriage, it was moving from California to Las Vegas that changed the trajectory of my life path.

In essence, it saved my life because it allowed me to take back my time because I became a contract worker for the company I worked for which then allowed me to work remotely from home and my hours were mine to decide on how much time to spend working and also how to schedule in more time for my marriage and quality time for myself.

I also decided then and there that I was going to start really leaning into living my life and not sitting on the sidelines anymore and that's when I started going to events and connecting with people and that then started me down my self-growth and self-love journey and I soon learned that not only did I love learning how to love myself and the life I was living, but also that it was something that I was passionate about teaching others to do and so began my journey into becoming a Life Coach for women.

So, circling back to my mom. Remember that I said that my mom gave me so much? Here's why I believe I am the woman that I am today. When I think about the words that I can say to express what my mom means to me, they are these: Brave, Loyal, Kind, Adventurous, Fearless, and Strong. Her strength helped me to find my own words and my courage to go out into the world forging my own destiny because she raised me to be a strong, confident, resilient, independent, brave, loyal, adventurous, and fearless woman, and because of the sacrifices she made, I have been able to go out into the world and lean into the uncomfortable spaces learning about myself and giving myself permission to be the person I choose to be, to do the things in life that I choose to do, and to have and lean into living the life I want to live.

Although the path has been precarious at times, I am grateful that I have been able to do the things that I am doing and that I am living a life of grace and gratitude.

Grace because I understand that I have to be in my story in order to write my story and that I don't have to be afraid of stepping into the uncomfortable spaces nor be afraid that I will mess up because I know that I can learn from my mistakes and use those lessons to be stronger and empower my Inner Hero.

Gratitude because I know that I am so very lucky to be living the life I am living and how I am living my life. I am so blessed for the people who have come into my life and who continue to bless me every day with their insights, support, and encouragement.

I know that life is not perfect and that the most beautiful things are revealed to us in our most imperfect moments in life. I believe to the core of my being that we are all born to add value to this world in our own individual, unique and beautiful ways and that we should never ever try to be someone else or something else that we are not because what we have to share may just be what someone else needs to hear. Our individual voices are just as important as they are joined together in community.

Along my journey, I learned that I have a Hero inside of me. We all do, and if we let her, our Inner Hero will guide us and love us and support us every step of our journey.

I know that it's not easy to love yourself wholly without judgment or criticism because it means being brave to look at your true reflection and getting real and honest and raw with yourself about your self-limiting beliefs and taking ownership for carrying them around with you as your truth.

I also believe that forgiveness is equally important as taking ownership and that forgiveness of self will allow you to release and move on and grow and become so much more than you could possibly imagine. Understand that we are human, and we are emotional beings, and that is a beautiful thing. We are deserving of so much if we just allow ourselves to believe.

When I realized that it was up to me to let go of my past, and that I could rewrite my story, it gave me the freedom to change how I lived. I took back my time and stepped into doing that which I love. It's my calling really. I love being a Coach! It has allowed me to work when I want, in the time that I choose, and to do this wonderful work wherever I choose to call my home. It has also allowed me to help transform the lives of the women that I have been blessed to work with, and who have given me the honor to work with them.

It has been enlightening and liberating to take back control over my time because time had been my master for so very long.

I have learned that time is a most precious commodity and that you can be a slave to your time OR you can use your time wisely and effectively and spend it living a life of fulfillment and joy.

If I can impart just a little bit of wisdom from my perspective, it would be these four things:

1. Don't ever let anyone tell you what your story is or should be. That's for you to decide.

2. Lean into the uncomfortable spaces, even when it gets scary, because when you allow yourself to be open to receiving, amazing things can reveal themselves to you.

3. Don't let anyone tell you your worth. The only person who is qualified to do that is You.

4. Embrace your Inner Hero and let her lead you and guide you because she loves you fiercely and loyally and wants only the best for you.

Last but not least, as you go through your life. Remember to navigate your day with an attitude of gratitude because with the right attitude, it will allow you to tackle life's curveballs or roadblocks when your emotional trigger moments happen.

Sending you much love and gratitude always!

Aileen V. Sicat

Lawyer | Educator | Writer | Spiritual Life Coach

https://www.linkedin.com/in/aileens

http://www.instagram.com/sheisaileens

https://rainbowswithaileen.com

Aileen V. Sicat gets to wear several hats---as lawyer, writer, educator, spiritual life coach among others. She hails from Metro Manila, Philippines.

Aileen was greatly shaped by her experiences as a graduate student in Japan and by her travels outside her home city. She aims to empower and to motivate people to continue to evolve into their best possible selves. As an intuitive coach, she uses modalities such as reiki, card readings (tarot and oracle), runes, numerology, astrology and a combination of some or all the above.

Aileen believes in dreams (with actions) and miracles.

From Fragile To Fierce

By Aileen V. Sicat

There is no going around it: I was fragile. Probably still a tad so and always will be. Yet I also managed to uncover the fierce side and allow it to shine whenever needed. It was quite a journey getting from one to the other and managing the in between.

What I learned along the way is that it is a choice to be unstoppable and one that we continue to make each day. I became unstoppable when I decided I chose to be. From then on, I never looked back.

AILEEN-o-CENTRIC

I am an only child and yes, my parents doted on me. A lot of our relatives did too, for various reasons. It was inevitable that I grew up in an *Aileen-o-centric* environment. Our home was about twenty minutes by car (given the traffic back then) to some of the prestigious universities in the country, so I never even had to leave home to attend university. It was a double-edged sword though. Along with the perks were imposed limitations that turned me into a sheltered young girl. I was used to things being handed to me on a silver platter. Hence, the fragility was emphasized.

Even as a young lawyer in a vintage, reputable law office, I was mostly pampered and treated like a fragile flower. I remember that a fatherly senior partner hesitated to send me to an enforcement operation that may escalate to something potentially violent. I insisted on going but I was allowed only when another male lawyer my age was sent along with me. I knew they meant well but it is suffice to say, the treatment did not help me grow to be independent.

Me, Myself and Aileen

The tides changed when I obtained a scholarship to pursue my Master of Laws (LLM) in Japan. In a whirlwind of activities, I found myself uprooting myself from my comfortable environment and living in a dorm room by myself.

Not only was I far from family and friends, I was also the only Filipina in my building and only one of three Filipinos in the seven buildings that made up the *ryugakusei kaikan* (the residence for foreign students).

The other two Filipinos in the building were undergraduate students below the age of 20. In Filipino culture, the elder siblings are naturally protective and nurturing of the younger ones even in adulthood. From being an only child, I found myself suddenly wearing big sister shoes. They also called me *"ate"* (pronounced *ahh-teh* which means elder sister) and treated me as such.

In my Master of Laws program, I was also the lone Filipino. On top of that, I was the first (and at that time the *only*) Filipino that a good number of my classmates met. I found myself realizing that the impression I would give them was bound to create an impact as to what many of them would think of Filipinos in general. I had to remind myself that I was a representative of my country and that I should be mindful of the responsibilities that came with it.

In hindsight, stepping outside my comfort zone paved way for most of my biggest milestones to date. Knowing that my actions reflected on my country emphasized my sense of purpose and motivated me to persevere.

Miss Independent

It may not be a big deal to many but doing things DIY (do it yourself) the Japanese way did not come easy for me. I was used to having help from family, house helpers and friends. Suddenly, I was doing everything by myself and figuring out how certain machines worked, being domesticated (somehow), and just doing my own thing. It was the start of my growth as a person. Learning how to do a lot of things my way, my style was cathartic even.

One thing that I still remember vividly was my experience of asking a Japanese lady how to use the photocopy machine. Everything was in Japanese and I could only understand hiragana and katakana plus maybe fifty out of thousands of kanjis at that point. The lady helped but she also asked me how I photocopied things in my country.

I told her there was a photocopy person who was in charge of doing the actual photocopying. The lady's surprise was evident. She could not fathom that there could be a job as a photocopy person or why it would even be necessary.

I also decided I wanted an *arubaito* (part-time job) while studying. I applied as an English teacher and started teaching Japanese of all ages. I had toddlers, grade schoolers, high schoolers, college students, lawyers and even a senior citizen who wanted to brush up on their English.

As one of the teachers in a language school, there were days I was singing out loud and thumping around with five-year olds and just thinking I was glad there was no recording of me looking that goofy. It was one for the books.

Late at night after three or four back-to-back teaching sessions, I found myself on a bus headed home to the *kaikan*, tired and hungry but fulfilled. The commute home gave me time to process how different my life in Japan was from driving to and from the office in my own car as I did back home. In Japan, I was not an administrator in a law school. The lawyer hat was not on and instead, I was a student, a part-time English teacher, a classmate, a foster sister, a friend. It was different and yet just as meaningful.

My Mini United Nations

I felt that I was on the way to bringing out the fierce side in me when I found myself finding fulfillment in helping my newfound friends affirm their uniqueness and renew their confidence. I realized it felt good to be on the giving end.

I met so many fabulous people in Japan who helped me grow as a person. I connected with people from all different walks of life and from different parts of the world. I remember the first few times we tried to eat as a group. Some people could not eat pork, some could not eat beef. There were other dietary restrictions brought about by either religion or health concerns. I was one of the people who could eat everything and anything, but I was also one of the pickier eaters. Finding a restaurant where everyone could have what they needed was a tad tricky.

The friendships I formed in Japan are special to me because I felt uninhibited with them. I was not Aileen the lawyer or the law lecturer who felt she had to be "proper" even when having fun. I was just myself.

As I went about my way being a listening ear to my friends and encouraging them to pursue their dreams, I realized it was time for me to do the same myself. The difference then was that at that point, I had to figure out what I really wanted. It was a matter of ascertaining things and going for it.

I found myself being less and less *Aileen-o-centric* as I focused on helping a few of my friends with different things each time. The adventures I had with them are worthy of a chapter or two in themselves, but it is suffice to say, as the focus shifted from myself to me being a means to help my friends and new sisters to succeed, I felt myself flourishing. My soul was fulfilled in ways it was not before. During my undergraduate years, we were always being shaped to be people for others. I really felt like I was during my time in Japan.

There was also this incident when my sister-like friend, Zakia, had to be taken to the hospital in an ambulance and a bunch of us rushed to be by her side. The nurse told me only family members were allowed. I politely but firmly asserted that we were all foreign graduate students there. We were all away from home. We were each other's family. The nurse asked me if I knew Zakia's date of birth with year. My other classmates did not know but fortunately, being the 'researcher' (a 'Nancy Drew' of sorts) that I was, I knew Zakia's details down to the year and was able to tell the nurse. After that, we were allowed to visit. Zakia saw us and felt loved. It was a beautiful moment.

Bearing Fruit

I gave my best in each academic activity. When it was announced that all those interested in presenting their working thesis at a symposium in Germany may submit proposals, I was among those who did. We were told that there might be a short list later on and those on it may be called for an interview. I had hoped my proposal would be considered.

I was already thinking of how I could possibly convince the professors that my topic should be chosen if I were to make it to the short list. On my birthday (my first and only birthday without any family with me), I received a magical email telling me I was chosen. I was headed for Germany as representative of that year's LLM batch.

I believe it was my pure intentions that got me chosen. I believe that many other topics may have been equally as interesting. We had judges, prosecutors and other high-ranking officials in their own companies and agencies in that batch. I believe though that when I submitted my proposal, I truly wanted to be chosen so I could talk about my topic with a wider audience that was also different from my usual ones. It was for the academic experience. I had talked to a few others who wanted the opportunity for the chance to visit Germany or to at least get away from the daily grind. For me, it was not even a consideration at that time. I honestly believe our intentions make a difference when all else may be equal.

VISA RUN(S)

Among those of us students headed for Germany, only I needed a visa. As I was sipping coffee at a Starbucks near the German Consulate during a day trip to deposit my documents, I felt fierce. I was getting used to doing things for myself, by myself and not minding that it was that way for me. I had stopped seeing myself at a disadvantage and had started to take challenges as opportunities for growth. Being the only one to need a visa was just part of the reality I had to face, and I chose to be an adult about it.

Just a month after I got back from Germany, there was another call for paper presentations that landed on my lap. This time it was for a university in Seattle, USA. Feeling inspired, I again submitted an entry. *Voila.* I soon received a letter of invitation to the workshop-presentation and was assured that my travel expenses were to be reimbursed and my accommodations taken care of. The gist for me was that it was time for another visa run and this time to the US Embassy.

Going for a visa application for the second time in a few weeks made me see how far I had gone and how I now looked forward to traveling to a new, unfamiliar setting by myself. *That* was progress.

TOKYO INTERN

I was also chosen to be an intern for a law firm in Tokyo just before graduation from LLM. Seeing first-hand how a successful firm in Tokyo operated was eye-opening and raised a lot of questions for me. Mainly, it made me re-assess what I wanted my legacy in life to be and what role lawyering had in it.

I realized that being unstoppable does not mean having all the answers. It can be simply knowing what questions to answer for yourself in order to make and sustain the choice to be unstoppable.

FINDING MY GROOVE

There is no one way to abide by the choice to be unstoppable. There will be challenges now and then. For me, I chose to keep seeing the bigger picture. As much as I loved the independence I found and the new me I unveiled in Japan, I knew that I would have to go back home. I would have to find ways to have the new and improved me fit in with the responsibilities that await me back home.

What I also knew was that I had to practice what I preached. I encouraged my friends to go after their goals. It was time I set my own and go after the same.

I graduated from LLM and returned home richer in friends and experience and with a lot of questions to answer for myself. I was on my way to making shifts happen for myself even if uprooting may be a bit painful.

FIERCE IS HERE TO STAY

Being in unfamiliar surroundings surely brought out the best in me. I discovered facets to myself that I never knew were there. I found out *I can. I will. I did.* I was unstoppable then and I can choose to be unstoppable in any setting I find myself in. I realized here are no such things as pigeonholed or too old, too ordinary or anything 'too'. Those are just perceptions. We can always shake things up if we want to and make changes as we see fit at any point in our lives.

I choose to take obstacles as challenges. I also choose to view redirections as forms of protection. There is always a silver lining to everything and there is always a tomorrow that awaits us. A 'no' to something we want may be what is best for us at this time even if we may not see it that way for now. There is always a higher purpose.

There is nothing wrong with being fragile or delicate. I did just fine when I was most of the time, but I evolved over time to having a touch of fierce. It was how I navigated life better as years went by. Not everyone has to be fierce to be unstoppable. Again, different strokes for different folks.

There are still times when I relish being in an *Aileen-o-centric* moment with family or dear friends, but I always manage to anchor myself to my higher purpose and not to center everything on myself, on what I need or what I want.

Fast forward to the present. I am not just doing lawyer work and teaching law nowadays. I am also pursuing my intuitive side, writing and coaching.

Yes, I had to step outside my comfort zone to grow as a person and to break free from just being fragile. I'm glad I did so. It is how I choose to be unstoppable.

Madison Tanner Clark

Founder Madison Tanner Media

www.instagram.com/madisontannermedia

www.madisontannermedia.com

Madison Tanner Clark, founder of Madison Tanner Media, is a professional copywriter who was born and raised in Miami, Arizona. She then moved to New York City for her undergraduate in Media, Culture, and the Arts. There she worked as a stage manager for several off-Broadway productions and spent over 5 years living and working there. Now Madison has her own writing company where she helps bloggers, marketing agencies, and influencers with their copy. She currently lives in Greensboro, North Carolina with her fur baby, Hollywood.

How We Keep The Faith With PTSD

By Madison Tanner Clark

To my mother, father, Lori Brockmeier, Sara DeLaney, and Jenna Mourey - you all taught me how to be a woman despite trauma.

On October 31, 2017, I took a walk around the Financial District to apartment hunt. I loved my life in New York City. I was about to graduate college in 6 short weeks and was planning to continue my life there. While sipping on an iced coffee, talking to my mother on the phone, walking around Battery Park staring at the Statue of Liberty, I counted my blessings. What other 21 year old gets to have a life like this?

I stepped out of the safe haven of Brookfield Place and into the crisp fall breeze, standing across from my favorite view of the city, the Freedom Tower. I smiled.

The smile quickly went away and was replaced with a gasp. My mouth unhinged as I watched grown men running in fear. "Madison? What's wrong?" I had forgotten I was on the phone with my mother. "Mom, something's wrong. People are running and screaming, I don't know what's happening." I heard her sigh and hesitantly she said, "You know what you have to do. Just keep me on the phone, please."

Before you think my mother is clinically insane for telling her only child to run into danger, she is a psychologist and my father was a detective. It was a household full of complete honesty and deliberate actions. They taught me to essentially be too aware of my surroundings and to fight instead of flight. To help instead of huddle. To save instead of being scared.

With that kind of experience under my belt, I took off in my 5-inch heels and sprinted harder than I ever had in my entire life. Not with the crowd, but against it. I zigzagged amongst parents holding their children dressed up in costumes. Children who were supposed to be excited for trick-or-treating, were instead being thrown over their parents shoulders in hopes of staying alive.

I almost didn't notice that there were now no cars on Battery Place. It was rush hour on a Tuesday in Downtown Manhattan. Something was *really* bad. I kept running and approached the police in a frenzy. They were working quickly to block off all the roads and I realized I was standing in the center of a crime scene. A stereotypical looking cop shouted at me, "What are you doing?" and without any hesitancy I yelled, "I'm with the press!" He didn't follow me and let me go through to what changed my life forever.

Laying on the sidewalk were bodies mangled up with bicycles they apparently had been riding. I was describing the scene to my mother as she, for once, was quiet and listened. I started snapping photos of the surrounding area as evidence.

As I'm taking pictures, I hear a man sobbing. I look frantically around and see a man just a few yards away from me laying on the ground, clearly distraught. It wasn't until I was on my knees next to him that I saw he had been run over, too. He grabbed my elbow, nearly yanking me down next to him, asking me where his brother was. "I-I don't know, sir. Where was he?" The man didn't hear me, he was too far into shock. "My brother! What happened to him?" I sat with this man as he screamed in pain and cried for his brother until EMTs appeared. The moment felt like hours but was a moment that turned into a newly minted memory that lives in my mind rent-free. He turned to me, "Let my brother know I'm okay, tell him where I'm going. Get my brother!" I nodded and told the man, "I will find him."

I never did and to this day, I don't know if that man or his brother made it.

Just hours after the longest 90 minutes of my life, I found a new side to myself as my brain chemically malfunctioned due to what I now know is post-traumatic stress disorder.

I will never forget that afternoon but I will also never forget that evening.

I had news outlets from all over the world calling my cell phone asking for the photos I took and if I had any videos. They were offering exorbitant amounts of cash that a senior in college would be stupid not to take. Although I did sell some photos of the ghost town that Downtown became, there was content I didn't. A woman from a media outlet called, "Oh honey, I am so sorry you had to witness that," then in the same breath asked, "Do you happen to have photos with bodies in it?" I hung up immediately. My rage grew thinking that people assumed I wanted to profit from murder. I was disgusted with how disassociated this world has become with death that they were willing to blast these lives lost on every screen across the world just to have a spicy story for the next two or three days.

Not long after that phone call, I had to go to an NBA game with my roommate that we had been wanting to go to for months. When I say "had to," I mean that I forced myself not to sit with what had just happened in hopes that maybe I could forget it and watch my hometown Suns play.

Taking our seats in Barclay Stadium, I wasn't prepared for another bout of rage to appear. There was a minute of silence for the terrorist attack and an update about the then body count. As most of us were silent, with tears in my eyes, I was disrupted by adults drunkenly laughing and throwing popcorn at each other just a few seats away. My eyes only saw red as I leaped up to attack, but my roommate grabbed me and threw me back into the seat. I snapped back to reality and started sobbing with anger and the realization that in a city of over 7 million people, probably no one else in that jam-packed stadium had seen what I had seen just hours earlier. I felt so alone.

That was my first glimpse into my new life with PTSD, but by no means was that going to be the last.

Sometimes that day feels like the climatic moment of a movie that I didn't ask to see. It feels too real one day, while some days I have to ask myself if that actually happened. Some days I get angry, some days I feel guilt. There are times where I ask God why He allowed me to be a witness to a terrorist attack, seeing lives lost in the name of evil. Why did I have to see a Home Depot rental truck veered in attempts to strike a school bus filled with happy, innocent, dressed up children on Halloween? Why did grown men run away while a 5 foot nothing 21-year-old ran to potentially fight the danger?

I still don't have all the answers as I write this.

My father begged me to go to therapy for years and I would make up countless excuses as to why I shouldn't. It wasn't until 2020 that I finally decided that I needed to, if not for his sake. I met the most kind, realistic therapist who was quick to assess my issues as PTSD.

Constant nightmares. Fits of rage. Intense emotions. Witnessing a traumatic event. Disassociation. Fear of death. Lack of trust in others. Never grieving and her favorite one that was icing on the PTSD cake, the part where I haven't spoken about it since it happened.

She was beyond certain that I had PTSD. It was clear as day to her in our first session. It was clear to my parents, my boss who had witnessed one of the most terrible events in human history, my roommates, and probably to others in my life. It was clear to everyone but me.

What I couldn't understand was one thing: how can I have PTSD when this is the type of thing that veterans are diagnosed with? I am not worthy enough to have such a heroic diagnosis. All I did was lie to the police, scared a few years out of my mother, and hold a strangers' hand that couldn't comprehend I was even there. I am no hero, I didn't save anyone's life. I was being a human being. I was being me. So why do I have a hero's post-war title?

It's taken a very long time to come to terms that PTSD is actually for everyone and most people have PTSD in some capacity. Whether you know it or not, many of your triggers that disrupt your psyche are connected to moments of trauma in your life. Thus having panic moments that you may or may not be aware of.

I'm not a medical professional, let's make that clear. Nonetheless, I have done my research with PTSD to learn more about how I can educate and care for myself so I can help others who are navigating through their new normal.

This chapter isn't to highlight my trauma in a glorified fashion. It isn't to make you feel guilty for not having witnessed what I have and have you contemplate if your traumas are "relevant," "valid," or are worthy of a PTSD diagnosis.

What this chapter is about is PTSD and your relationship with it, whatever that may look like. Trauma does not have to be seeing evil, death, and war. Trauma is what you have gone through that has changed your brain's balance that has given you triggers and what some of us call baggage.

The most common description of post-traumatic stress disorder is the following: PTSD is a disorder in which a person has difficulty recovering after experiencing or witnessing a terrifying event.

What I have learned is that PTSD can come from anything. A car accident, a divorce, a miscarriage, an abusive relationship, your childhood, chemo treatment, the loss of a pet, being triggered when receiving an email, and even financial difficulties.

Just like most other mental illnesses, PTSD does not look like one certain thing. Which I had to nail into my brain for years. Ultimately, if you have gone through an event in your life that still causes you to be triggered, have panic attacks, or have nightmares about - congratulations, you have PTSD.

But living with PTSD doesn't have to be impossible. It doesn't have to be something that you see on someone's face the moment you see them. It doesn't have to be crippling, it doesn't have to mean you have to be monitored by healthcare professionals. It means that you have another day to share your story of resilience by living your life.

That isn't to say that you won't have days of being in a really bad mood and not consciously knowing that your brain knows what today is while you don't remember its significance. You will have days where you will forget the event altogether but then something someone says, something you see on your drive, something from a song lyric pops up, and you go into a spiral where you are experiencing a panic attack in the middle of a Whole Foods.

Yeah, PTSD is tricky like that.

Before my own experience, there was the Manchester bombing that happened right outside an Ariana Grande concert and in later years she shared brain scans of her brain before and after the event. By the time she shared these images, my event had already happened. Even though the images are heartbreaking, it gave me a sense of relief and understanding that I'm not holding onto this event for my own ego. My brain literally changed and has its own difficulty processing the event.

Your PTSD is not you wanting attention. It is not you thinking you are being too sensitive. It is not you thinking you can't process your feelings or thoughts. It is not you wanting to hold onto the past. Your PTSD has nothing to do with you and everything to do with your brain and the chemical reactions that occurred after your traumatic event.

However, this isn't an excuse to be like, "I have PTSD so I'm allowed to be a dick when I want to." Yeah, I'll never condone that. You are allowed to have your ebbs and flows of emotions, but you are not allowed to use your mental illness as an excuse for your naturally bad attitude.

Keeping the faith with PTSD can be hard. It can be one of those things where you want to power through it and pretend like it never happened. It can also be one of those things where you feel like it is controlling your life.

But I am here to tell you that how you choose to go about managing your PTSD is up to you and how your brain and body best responds to it. This can mean that every year on the anniversary you do a little something. You can take prescribed medications. You can talk with a therapist, friends, or family. You might be one of those people with a really kind brain that is able to pull an Elsa and let it go. None of these options are better or worse than one another. Just because you talk with a therapist and have to be on medications does not mean you are weak. If you pick up a dozen tulips on the anniversary every year, it does not mean you're not letting it go. All of these ways are valid and you can heal yourself anyway it works for you.

Whatever your experience is or was, your PTSD is valid and a scar that many of us will carry for the rest of our lives. But guess what? That is okay.

Our stories help remind others that they are not alone. It gives people the space to talk to someone who might be able to empathize with their struggles. Your story might be the reason why someone can believe they can keep going because you do. And because of everyone that I mentioned at the beginning of my chapter and their stories of trauma, I was able to keep the faith with my PTSD.

This one's for you. The ladies who are unstoppable beyond human comprehension. The women who are PTSD warriors. The female heroes that each of us know in our lives who are able to walk on through life with confidence despite their PTSD. You all inspire everyone around you even when you're in bed crying after a terrible nightmare. You are so strong, so loved, so empowered.

For the young Madison that didn't know that Halloween 2017 was going to change that fun-loving holiday forever, you've gotten so much stronger than you ever thought possible. Let people in, let people help you, and you cry about everything else, so it's okay to cry about this every now and then when you want to.

That is how we keep the faith with PTSD.

God gave you the power to do what you cannot do
Every road we travel He's traveled down before
There ain't no need to worry where it leads to anymore
I'm walkin' on.

Lovely LaGuerre

Founder Pure Heavenly Hair Boutique

https://www.linkedin.com/company/pure-heavenly-hair

https://instagram.com/pureheavenlyhair

https://m.facebook.com/Pure-Heavenly-Hair-Boutique-107278091130735

www.PureHeavenlyHair.com

www.LovelySellsVegas.com

Lovely LaGuerre is an entrepreneur, #1 international best-selling author of The Successful Woman's Mindset 21 Journeys to Success, a licensed commercial and luxury real estate agent. She is on a mission to help you turn your real estate investment dreams into a reality. She is also the Founder of Pure Heavenly Hair Boutique, a luxury beauty brand transforming, inspiring and empowering women to unleash their beauty inside and out. She is a member of NAIOP, CALV, NAR, GLVAR Association, Wealthy Women Inner Circle and many more! She resides in Las Vegas with her loving family.

Leading With Purpose: My Vision, My Reality

By Lovely LaGuerre

- Finding Inspiration -

There are plenty of reasons as to why you've found yourself reading this here today. Perhaps you wish to learn more about the entrepreneurial world or gather insights to the author's life. Whatever the case may be, I am going to begin by explaining the utmost factor that you need to learn before starting with your entrepreneurship.

Whatever you do in life, be it as little as crossing something off your to-do list, or bringing one of your ideas to life, finding inspiration to do so is the primary goal. As simple as it may sound, finding motivation to carry out any task is one of the most challenging things to do out there. Sure, you may have some totally brilliant idea for a new start-up business, but what is your source of inspiration? What inspires you to follow your dreams and achieve the goals you long to achieve? Answering these questions in your mind before taking the big step towards this new chapter in your life, is the only way you can assure your success.

Finding inspiration has a lot to do with finding out who you are. Although, this might sound quite simple. In fact, you would be shocked to find out how many individuals searching for their uniqueness and why they're doing what they are. In order to explore and know more about yourself, a good idea would be to keep a diary. Noting down all the ideas that you get in your brain regarding your new business, what triggers them, and how they make you understand is a spectacular idea to get to know yourself better.

An important factor to keep in mind before setting out to seek inspiration is to let yourself loose. If you're constantly on the hunt to find inspiration, chances are you perhaps might never be able to find that IT factor. Inspiration can come to you at any point of the day, wherever you are, and whatever time it may be. You can find it either sitting on your bed and thinking about your entrepreneurship dream, you can find it by watching something on television, by reading something in a book or simply being in a quiet setting. Make it a habit to research on anything and everything you come across.

Once you dig into the details and get to know more about something, it might give you plenty of new ideas, while boosting up your creativity. Moreover, stepping out of your comfort zone, getting out of your own way, experimenting, and learning more about a world you do not know is going to help you launch your career significantly.

Once you discover what inspires you to start your venture, you will become unstoppable. During bad days when you have nothing to look forward to, or no reason to continue doing what you are, your inspiration is going to help you achieve your goals and is going to stop you from giving up. In fact, giving up will not even be an option in front of you, when you have a clear source of inspirations for your goals the potential can be infinite.

-Taking the First Step-

As we've heard our entire lives, "Taking the first step is always the hardest." Have you ever stopped to ponder upon what it meant? Sure enough, we do take a lot of steps in our lives, but what's most important is the **first step**. To take the first step, it does not just require the willingness, but there are several other significant factors at ploy behind it.

Let's look at a few reasons as to why you might delay taking the first step. Oftentimes, we wait for the *perfect moment.* We don't appreciate things for the way they are at the time being, but instead, we wait for them to get better and better, as if we're live in an ideal world. I learned this the hard way, but there is no *perfect moment*. It's merely an illusion our mind has created, in order to delay or stop you from achieving your goals. No matter how good the moment is, your mind will never accept it as *perfect*, so take that step right now. Filter all those thoughts and illusions from your mind and do what you've been waiting for all this time.

Most aspiring entrepreneurs are often *perfectionists*. They believe that each step they take must be calculated, planned, and flawless. In order to perfect whatever ideas they get in their brains, they spend a considerable amount of time just obsessing over the tiny details, rather than making it happen. If you're one of these people, you need to kill that habit right away.

While it's an exceptional quality to brainstorm and put all your ideas down on paper and make calculations, knowing when to put your thoughts and plans into actions is crucial to be successful. Don't spend an entire lifetime for planning something, and yet not taking actions.

When I recall my initial days of starting up my business, I remember staying up all night, penning down the costs of the equipment I needed to get started. I would research them on various platforms and find them to be extremely expensive, or way out of the budget I had set for them. However, after all those plans, I decided to step out one day and see for myself if I could get the equipment in some way. As I took my first step, I even took a small risk by using a portion of my savings to invest towards something that I believed in.

The reason why I tell this story is to give the readers, you, a source of inspiration that you never know what's in store for you until you step out and see for yourself. Make that first move right now, you have planned enough, and achieve whatever you've been planning so much for. Sometimes, it's true that taking a step might be risky, or wouldn't go as you might have planned in your *perfectionist* diary, but you never know until you actually try.

When you look back at this time, the only thought that will come to your mind is going to be, "why didn't I take this step earlier?" As pivotal it is to wait for the right moment, you should also know when to put your pen down, and your foot up, to set out for what you wish to achieve.

-Being Consistent-

Consistency is the key to success. We have heard this phrase numerous times repeatedly, and on various occasions. Is it that easy as casually as people say it is? I beg to differ.

Now that you have taken your first step to achieve your dreams, the success of your entrepreneurship solely depends on the actions you take from this moment on. In order to start being consistent with your hard work for your entrepreneurship, you must know the reason as to why you need to be consistent in the first place.

So many individuals do certain things in life, such as going to their daily jobs, but they never know why they do so. Well, once you find out why you're doing something, life becomes ten times easier for you. Each time you feel like giving up, that reason is going to show up in front of you and give you ten more reasons in your head to become unstoppable. So, why should you be consistent again?

Let's take the example of a flower or plant for instance. You get the seeds from someplace, that's your equipment right there. You put the seed in the soil, and then you water it. That's the next step you take in order to start the growth of the plant, a lot like your business. What's next? You water the soil and the seed every day, depending upon its needs and requirements. You take a certain quantity of water, and you pour it all over the soil and you do it daily. Consistently.

If you skip the watering process for even one day, the plant dries up. The tips and edges of the leaves dry out or turn brown. That means, if you stop being consistent for just one day, your hard work and consistency of all the previous days are put in jeopardy too. Imagine what would happen if you watered the plant consistently every day? It will blossom and grow into its best version.

Well, entrepreneurship is somewhat similar. If you're promoting your business on an everyday basis, that's remarkable. However, let's suppose you don't promote your business one day due to tiresome or an unknown reason? and this day turns out to be that day when potential clients are looking for leads in your business niche? All your labor of love and efforts are somewhat wasted, just because you could not work that one day.

To conclude, consistency is the key to success. Whatever strategies you follow, whatever plans you create, and whatever measures you decide to take will be ineffective if you don't follow them on an everyday basis, and if you aren't consistent. Entrepreneurship is not easy, and that is why the outcomes are so generous.

You will face hardships, and some adversities in your entrepreneurial journey, however if you take on all these challenges with solidity and hard work, you can be relentless most importantly unstoppable. Moreover, the more you practice in mastering your crafts, the more enriched you become. So, with consistency, you're not just paving your way to success, but you're also becoming exceptional at what you do.

-Believing in Yourself-

The most significant part of your entrepreneurship is you. You are the brains, the muscle, the tools, you are your everything. In order to keep a successful entrepreneurship, having a strong belief in yourself is not just essential, but crucial.

There are going to be a lot of times where you might doubt yourself or your capabilities, where you might feel like there's no way out, and in such times, all you're going to require is a solid principle. Having faith in yourself and knowing that you are enough taps into your genius zone and carrying out all your responsibilities perfectly will enable you to move forward successfully.

A strong belief in oneself and an unshakable faith are attributes that are co-related with other attributes as well. One such attribute would be self-confidence. If you have self-awareness and enough confidence in yourself to be able to execute something perfectly, then you will be able to accomplish everything. The greatest enemy of a human being, and the best friend of a human being, is their mind. The way a particular human's mind operates is the determining factor of whether or not that human will achieve success.

Many aspiring entrepreneurs hesitate to make decisions or to take big steps due to the fear of failure. Or when they do take a certain step and fail, they let that failure control them and their mindset. Instead of moving on to bigger plans and continuing to stay laser focused, these individuals tend to obsess over their failures. However, it is imperative to know when to not pay heed to such failures, and move on forward with the hopes to improve, expand your horizons.

As an individual, and especially as women, we get to face a lot of challenges against ourselves. People try to question our capabilities, or think of us as 'relatively unsuccessful', but we must not pay heed to this. The only obstacle we need to battle is our mind.

Along with self-belief and faith, we need to learn to prioritize ourselves. As entrepreneurs, we have a lot of things going on in our lives. We must learn to create the perfect balance between our professional and personal lives. In order to be a master at balancing these, making a schedule for your daily chores seems like a brilliant idea. Set some time apart for your personal life, family, and friends. Use this as quality time to find yourself and your anchor.

The remaining time you need to set apart is for your entrepreneurship. Decide a certain number of hours you want time blocked and follow them religiously. Most of the times, the hours are not entirely fixed, and vary depending upon the nature of your tasks, so manage that accordingly. Whatever you do, just don't waste time on things that are not of value. Most importantly, learn how to prioritize yourself.

Your social and professional life will keep going on, but then again taking care of yourself and your mental peace is just within your hands. Set out Sundays for a self-care day, where you spend the entire day treating yourself, relieving yourself from all the stress, and just regaining your mental peace. Running an entrepreneurship can get hectic and exhausting for your mind, and you must give yourself a break whenever you feel like it's too much. Overworking yourself is definitely not a healthy habit. Work hard enough to ensure that all your goals are met, but don't overwork yourself in the hopes of achieving success fairly quicker. Remember, your health is of greater significance than your entrepreneurship. Don't lose yourself overachieving success.

Updating your Goals -

As the title of this chapter insinuates, updating your goals is an important step to ensure your long-term success. As discussed in chapter one, we find a source of inspiration for ourselves to keep going on. Then the question arises, how long does this inspiration last? Is it enough to keep you motivated throughout your entire life? Perhaps not.

When we start off by making our decisions and aligning our goals, we usually make short term goals. In the entrepreneurial world, the most successful people are those who make rational decisions, that not only cause benefits to their entrepreneurships, but also secures them for the long-term. One trait that a successful entrepreneur must have to make practical decisions quickly. This is due to the fact that any decision made by the entrepreneur can make or break the company or business. Along with making the right decisions, the timing of the decision-making is crucial. Some decisions have to be made at the right time, or when the circumstances fit best, and an effective entrepreneur must know when to step out of their comfort zone and take that big step when it's time.

Coming back to your goals, it's absolutely essential to keep your goals updated from time to time to keep yourself motivated. For instance, when you first started your entrepreneurship, your first goal must've been to purchase a nice car for yourself, or a new house. Well, what happens once you've achieved that for yourself? What new goals do you have to look forward to?

It's essential to always have something to look forward to, so that you perform your tasks and everyday chores with the contentment of your heart. Keep your goals updated, and always have something new to look forward to. Doing so will only help you stay motivated.

A question that most readers will have after reading this is, "how often should we update our goals?" Well, to answer that question, it depends on the nature of your goals, and the rate at which you're succeeding. If you're achieving the initial goals you have set for yourself, it's time to update them and create new ones.

When we talk about stepping out of the comfort zone, it is imperative to get out of your own way and make a shift that will determines the direction of your career. As women, there are hundreds of ifs and don'ts that come in our way, however if we learn to strengthen ourselves and our mindset enough to set the right goals for ourselves, we will be unstoppable.

Your aspirations take you to success and define who you will be. So, take a deep breath and factor in what you want to achieve in life. Believe in yourself, aim at your new goals and write them all down, grant yourself of what is needed and trust your journey. Cross off your old goals that you have achieved and be proud of what you've become. Set up new strategies and ideas to achieve your new desired goals and start working accordingly for immeasurable results.

- Maintaining your Success -

If you keep your hard work consistent, you can definitely achieve success in your entrepreneurship. The biggest challenge you will face, however, is to maintain your success.

We all can establish the fact that a person tends to not work as hard once they achieve success. The peak of the hard work of the person is from the initial point of when they start working for their entrepreneurship to the point when they start receiving the benefits of their success. So, in this case, how does one maintain their success?

First and foremost, keep a written plan. Your previously written plan may be achieved, so remember to update it. Update your plan and come up with new strategies for your entrepreneurship. Plan it all out. To maintain your success, it's important to know what you're doing and what you must do.

Make edits in your plan where necessary. You don't need to have one adamant plan which you stick to for life. Keep making changes and adapting according to situations and circumstances.

Always listen to what your close ones have to say. If you don't take second opinions from people close to you, you will not be able to maintain what you have built.

One of the most important factors that you need to adopt in yourself is not have too much pride within yourself. Being proud of your accomplishments and achievement of goals is one thing but taking too much pride and being egoistic over your achievements is considered a negative attribute. Whatever you do, always stay humble to the people around you. If it weren't for them, you probably wouldn't even be at this place.

Other than being humble, always remember to be grateful. Don't look at people who are way more successful than you and frown. Instead, be grateful for whatever you have achieved and strive hard to do better, and to reach a place higher than where you are right now.

Remember to keep track of whatever you do, the numbers are your best friends, so always keep yourself updated on them. The only way to ensure success in the long-term and to maintain it is to keep a constant track of anything and everything. Don't become absent after working hard and continue to work with the same energy you had since the first day.

It's quite challenging to work with the same enthusiasm and energy, but this is when the inspiration comes to play. If you have a strong source of inspiration, and your goals are updated, nothing can come in your way. Remember to stay focused and have a look at your goals each day before starting to work, it'll help you focus and do better.

With that, I conclude my book chapter and I hope it served as a ray of inspiration and motivation for you to kickstart your entrepreneurship. If you have made it until here, you're completely ready to step into the entrepreneur world and achieve all the success you've dreamt of. From this moment, the only way is forward and upward!

Charlotte Howard Collins

Business Breakthrough Strategist | Award-Winning Publisher | Book Publicist | Best Selling Author | Speaker | Entrepreneur | Founder, Wealthy Women Inner Circle Executive Producer, Wealthy Women Entrepreneurs Network

www.instagram.com/coachwithcharlotte

www.facebook.com/coachwithcharlotte

www.linkedin.com/coachwithcharlotte

www.iamcharlottehoward.com

Charlotte Howard Collins is a world class business growth expert who helps female authors, female entrepreneurs, beauty salon professionals and women business owners build successful and profitable businesses doing what they love. She teaches things that are beyond college education. Her journey from working as a full-time licensed hairstylist employee to becoming a successful female entrepreneur has inspired more than 5000 women globally to build their own businesses. Her Hair Artist Association has more than 4,000 members. She has received numerous awards including Top

Transformational Women Leader Award and Extraordinary CEO'S To Watch Award! Charlotte and her team have helped clients create awareness for their books through various strategies including book reviews, articles, feature stories, mentions, radio interviews, tv interviews and more! They have successfully launched more than 1000 International Best Selling Books in 13 different languages. To learn more visit

www.iamcharlottehoward.com ,
www.heartcenteredwomenpublishing.com and
www.thehairartistassociation.org

Clarity Leads To Cash Flow

By Charlotte Howard Collins

Are you ready to become an unstoppable woman personally and professionally? Let me share with you the secrets that helped me to create my very own unstoppable path and how you can too!

The world of business is fast-paced. Whether you are running an established business or just starting one, you will always look for innovative ways to grow your enterprise and improve the bottom line. While building a business for yourself or helping people is an admirable goal, it is far from easy.

Especially if the business' primary agenda is helping other businesses. It is one thing to solve an industry's problem or come up with a unique product. To have a social impact or to bring a dramatic change in other businesses, that calls for something special. You must have clarity to become an unstoppable woman in your life and business.

My unstoppable journey started in the year 2000 after my carpal tunnel syndrome diagnosis, my life was rapidly altered. I decided not to undergo surgery and went for natural options and had incredible success throughout my life. The major roadblock was people who did not approve of my methods and wanted me to return to a 9-5 job.

Some of these people included friends and family who didn't think it was an achievement for me to continue the journey and become an entrepreneur. They only cared for the old ways, thinking that a career can only be stable through a job. For me, the greatest lesson was not to listen to people letting me down, because I knew I could do anything I put my mind to.

Overcoming all these struggles, I created an unstoppable approach to living as a 7-Figure Woman Entrepreneur with multiple businesses. I have clarity that led to cash flow and a happy and fulfilling life.

The best thing to hold onto in life is each other. I am approaching my 42nd birthday on September 12, 2021. I thank God for the blessings. I am now happily married to my loving and supportive husband Russell Collins two decades of memories, but we are going to make more. We have four beautiful and supportive kids Daija Howard, Daivontae Howard, Destiny Howard and Da' Kari Howard that we are extremely proud of. I have supportive family, friends and clients that I love with all my heart. I pursued my mission to help women heal, thrive, and grow personally and professionally with confidence.

I now teach female authors, female entrepreneurs, beauty salon professionals and women business owners how to create clarity so they can generate more clients, close more sales and increase their overall revenue and profits. I guide them on a transformational journey to live their dream lives using the power of publishing.

To become an unstoppable woman, you must always be open to fresh experiences with the many titles and roles you play. An unstoppable woman always exercises fairness to others, no matter what. An unstoppable woman cares about people beyond her inner circle of influence and gives back to others. An unstoppable woman carries an inspiring, outgoing personality, spreads positivity everywhere she goes, and always encourages others.

If you want to have a happy and fulfilling life doing what you love, stand out from the crowd, and embrace the unstoppable woman you are becoming by sharing your unique story.

Step 1: What's Your Why?

The first step in your journey to becoming an unstoppable woman in life and business is to discover your "why." This is an essential question that women must be able to answer. Your why might be as simple as more money or more free time, or it might be as complex as wanting to start a charity or spend summers on mission trips.

Some ideas to get you started:

- I want to spend more time with my husband and kids while they're little

- I want to home-school my children and I can't do that if I work outside the home

- I want to support my parents as they age

- I want the freedom to travel

- I want to support a charity that's close to my heart

- I want to live a certain lifestyle

- I want to write a book

What does any of this have to do with becoming an unstoppable woman? Everything!

When you define your unique "why" you will be able to build a life and business that you truly love and that you are passionate about. That's why so many female entrepreneurs and business owners feel like a failure at a job, they simply aren't passionate and it doesn't feed their "why."

Only you have that power, and it's up to you to discover your unique meaning in life, so you can build a life and business that allows you to achieve your goals.

The best way to discover your why is to create a vision board. It's easy, fun and gives female entrepreneurs and business owners a fabulous way to visualize those dreams and help make them a reality.

Here's what you'll need:

- Colored pencils or markers

- Old magazines

- Colored paper, ribbon, or Washi tape

Begin by browsing through your magazines and cutting out any pictures that appeal to you. You can also gather pictures of your family, friends, favorite vacations or anything else that will help define what you want your ideal life to look like.

Arrange your images on a large piece of paper. Get creative with notes, goals, favorite quotes, or anything else that helps inspire you. Then post your completed vision board on your office wall, where you'll see it every day and where it will serve as a constant reminder of why you do what you do.

Step 2: Your Story Matters

Along with your "why," comes your story. Your unique background will appeal to your ideal client in a way that no one else's will. Again, we're not necessarily talking about business here (we'll get to that story in the next step) but instead, we want to focus on your personal life.

- What struggles have you overcome?

- What hardships have you faced?

- How have you impacted someone else's life?

- How has another person impacted you?

Everyone struggles at some point, and when you meet your ideal client in Step 4, she will resonate with your story, and you might just become her inspiration. Where no other person has been just the right fit, you will be.

Using the questions in my chapter, spend an hour (or more) writing your story. Share the details of your life, why you chose this business model, and how that affects your clients and customers. What in your background makes you the perfect coach for your ideal client?

Please be as detailed and forthcoming as you can. No one will read this but you, but it's important to know what truly drove you to start your business. You'll be sharing bits and pieces of this story in the months and years to come, and it will help connect you to your ideal client.

Step 3: Write Your Mission Statement

At its most basic, your mission statement defines who you are, what you do, and for whom. Potential customers should be able to read your mission statement and immediately know whether or not you're a good fit.

A well-thought-out mission statement is so much more important than that. It's the point on the horizon that will keep you focused. It's the litmus test to which every new idea or strategy must stand up and it has everything to do with your unique story.

You may choose to use your mission statement on your website, in your marketing materials, as your tagline, or elsewhere. At the very least, print and post it near your desk, where you will be able to see it every day. You can keep it completely to yourself, using it as a "touchstone" to guide every business-related decision.

Thinking of creating a new self-study program? Consider branching out into a related area? Intrigued by a hot new social platform? Test it against your mission statement first, and you'll instantly know if it's something you should pursue.

Your mission statement will also help you make difficult decisions about potential clients. Sometimes clients come our way who simply aren't an ideal fit, and by carefully considering them in light of your mission statement, you'll be able to easily see the truth.

Here's a basic template you can use, but feel free to write it your way, in your voice and style:

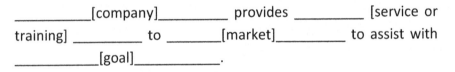

_____[company]_____ provides _____ [service or training] _____ to _____[market]_____ to assist with _____[goal]_____.

Step 4: Your Unique Offer

Here's where a lot of female entrepreneurs and women business owners get stuck: Determining your "USP" or Unique Selling Proposition.

In other words, what sets you apart from all the other entrepreneurs, service providers, trainers, and product sellers out there? Why would someone buy from you, when there are so many other choices?

The answer is simple, really: Because none of those other people are you!

None of them have your personality.

None of them have your experience.

None of them have your insights.

Also none of them have your story.

Truthfully, it's that last one that will really resonate with your ideal client. By sharing your story in an authentic, personable way, you'll make an immediate connection with your audience.

Maybe you overcame a hardship and eventually found success in your field. This will encourage others like you to reach a little further. Maybe you taught yourself a complex marketing strategy through trial and error and can now share your knowledge with others who are also struggling. Or maybe you've had the privilege of training with high-end, well-known experts in your industry, and now feel ready to lead as well.

Whatever your unique story is, there are those for whom it will resonate like no one else's will. Remember, we can hear the same advice time and time again, but it won't really sink in until we hear it in just the right way, from just the right person.

And for a certain audience, that someone is you.

Ask yourself these questions, and really think about the answers. Don't worry about saying the right thing or writing like this is a sales page. Just share from your heart. You'll eventually want to use this information in your sales pages and other marketing materials, but right here is just for you.

1. What has been your biggest struggle in business? In life? How did you overcome it?

2. What was your biggest "win" in business? How did you celebrate?

3. What's your biggest regret in business?

4. What's your biggest business goal? Life goal? How do you plan to achieve your goals?

Thank you for reading my chapter in this phenomenal book. I want to help you create your own unstoppable woman success system. I created my signature success system entitled clarity leads to cash flow. It goes much deeper than what I shared in my chapter and it's designed to help you take your life and business to the next level. If you want access visit www.iamcharlottehoward.com and inquire about my system.

Please remember to leave this book a review on Amazon. When you do leave a review email me at info@iamcharlottehoward.com for unannounced bonus exclusively from me.

Alicia L. O'Neal M.Ed

The Posh Veg Owner and Healthy Eating & Lifestyle Coach

https://www.linkedin.com/in/alicia-oneal3

https://www.instagram.com/theposhveg

https://www.facebook.com/theposhveg

https://www.theposhveg.com

Facebook Group (Happy & Healthy Boss Women):
https://www.facebook.com/groups/happyandhealthybosswomen

Alicia O'Neal is a small town girl from Anderson, Indiana, with a heart for big city life. She earned her B.S. in Biology & Society from Cornell University with focuses in Nutrition & Health, Science & Technology Studies, and Education. Additionally, she earned a M.Ed in Higher Education with research in Health Education from Arizona State University, and is currently earning her P.hD in Population Health (Cancer Research) from the University of Kansas School of Medicine. With more than 7 years of clinical, research, hospital, and teaching experience, her passions lie at the intersection of being happy and healthy and supporting other women to do the same. Her business, The Posh Veg, aims to help women find food, body, and emotional freedom through science-based physical and mental support. In her free time, she's likely traveling, meditating, reading, spending time with family/friends, or cooking tasty meals.

Healing From The Inside Out

By Alicia O'Neal

If you would've told me that before turning 25, I'd be invited to write a chapter in a book called, "Becoming an Unstoppable Woman", I don't know if I would have believed it. I'm still a bit stunned in all honesty, but I guess this is what happens when you're a small-town girl, who's never had small dreams.

So how did I get here, you ask? It all started in a small town, Anderson, Indiana where I realized pretty quickly that I love to learn and that I was pretty good at it too. My parents raised my brother and I to be in a never ending state of learning, even when we were toddlers, from reading signs aloud while in the car, to reading the origin stories of all the animals at the zoo, to growing older and having homework every day during the summer, to giving countless church speeches, creating next level school projects, and ultimately leaving home to go to college across the country, we were made for this quite honestly.

Many people are baffled when I say that even after attending med camp, graduating high school with a 4.7 GPA, and getting into multiple Ivy League schools, I didn't even consider myself to be smart. I had always recognized that I was different, but when your high school graduating class only had 65 people, it was easy to see everyone was unique. Learning was just a part of who I was. I think when I started teaching courses at Cornell and then landed a clinical internship at the Icahn School of Medicine of Mount Sinai Hospital in New York City, after being rejected more than I can count, it finally clicked for me. I was really proud of myself, I had worked so hard to land that internship. Only then, did it really hit me that my normal was nowhere close to the norm. At that point, I was 21 years old, I had been a college cheerleader, was nearly a Cornell graduate, a woman of Delta Sigma Theta Sorority, Inc., and a creator of tangible change on campus alongside Cornell's administrators. Becoming unstoppable was instinctive, to a degree.

After graduating from Cornell, I moved across the country, again, to Arizona State University this time. I earned my masters in Higher Education and spent a great deal of time working in NIH funded labs, researching nutrition and health, chronic diseases, and health behavioral influences for college students. Arizona was also the place where I created The Posh Veg, my healthy eating and lifestyle business. I never imagined myself as an entrepreneur, but from my love of food, a business that helps women find food, body, and emotional freedom using scientific methods for physical and mental healing has blossomed.

At this point, I'm less than two years away from earning my PhD from a medical school and my brother's running joke that I'm a "school lifer" rings pretty true. What I've realized is that while I love to learn, my learning has come just as much from inside the academic setting, as it has outside of it.

I think most people see my life from the outside and think I don't have any failures. That it's just pristine and perfect. That I've gotten here without as much of a simple headache or scrape. That I don't make mistakes and that's simply not true. I've had a lot of moments of big struggle. From failing multiple classes at Cornell, to being chronically depressed throughout college, to digging myself DEEP in debt because I wasn't wise with my money, or even being bedridden for two and a half months after randomly becoming sick.

The hard truth is: at a certain point, being unstoppable is a choice. To keep moving no matter what. To take steps even when life has you down, bad, I mean worse than you've admitted to anybody else. That can be soul crushing sometimes, defeating even... to need a win so bad, LOSE, and then choose to try again, again and again. Then an infinite amount of times after that too.

That experience isn't pretty. It's quite ugly, in fact. If you're at all like me... you're a crier. I mean big crocodile tears popping up in the most inconvenient moments. Funny thing is, I used to be embarrassed that I'd cry even over the smallest things, until I was playing a game with one of my mentors in college. She just paused, looked me dead in the eyes and said aloud "I cry almost every day. It's just one of the ways I express myself".

This is a woman who is strong, fierce, fun, brilliant, charismatic, I mean a true force to be reckoned with, and she just admitted that she opens the floodgates regularly, with no inhibition. There's a lot of strength in that. Too many people are afraid to sit with their emotions. I mean really connect with them, see them, feel them. The excitement, the shame, the disappointment, the pride, the frustration. All of it, good and bad. For me, that means that my tear ducts just get a bit more exercise than other people. Now this doesn't mean you have to let everyone else see your tears, or have a tell all every time something happens. Nobody has time for that. Literally, there are too many things that happen in a single day, week, let alone life but, it does mean that you should know your needs and lean into tending to them.

The beautiful thing though is that, when I started to allow myself to cry when I really needed it, it unlocked my capability to experience life in a more brilliant way. Not only did it actually reduce my tendency to make mountains out of molehills, but it also helped me become more resilient. When I accepted that unfortunate things may arise in life, they no longer had that "time freeze" impact on me. Most importantly, I started laughing A LOT more. I realized that my life deserved laughter, in every phase, good or bad.

There is a verse in the Bible that my parents store is based upon and it's stayed with me for a while. Ecclesiastes 3:1 says, "For everything, there is a season, a time for every activity under heaven." The scripture then elaborates on all sorts of different types of seasons we will experience throughout life, but one that is particularly relevant for me is verse 2b where it says there is, "A time to plant and a time to harvest." To me, that is a huge factor in my ability to become unstoppable even before I lived a quarter century, understanding that as a student, a business woman, and young adult, most of what I am doing is planting seeds for my future harvest.

I'm from what they call "the microwave generation", researchers characterize us as wanting everything within an instant or short waiting period. I understand the desire for instant gratification. It can be hard to put in work, effort, or energy, and not see an immediate return. In a way, it almost feels like failure or rejection even. Especially with social media, seeing people buy new cars, jet set around the world, get married, or even celebrate the smallest moments in their lives can be triggering when you feel like you're stuck, or life isn't going the way you want.

The important thing to remember about social media is that it's all a projection. People only share what they want you to see, what they feel proud of, what they feel good about, what makes them laugh, or what makes them feel motivated. It's nearly all done out of self-interest. Which is totally okay, but also why I had to distance myself for nearly two years. I was becoming an unstoppable woman prior to my social media hiatus, but it helped me have the space to think clearly without feeling pressure to always "report out" what I was doing, where I was going, or how life was treating me because at times, it was treating me pretty badly.

With all my reflection in this chapter, I want you to remember that I am still planting. I have harvested, but I am still planting. The process is never ending, that's the whole point of being unstoppable, and as you plant more intentionally and wisely, your harvest will become more frequent.

As we progress through this chapter, I hope you receive whatever it is you need, a jolt, push, pivot, or encouragement to engulf yourself in a season of planting for your harvest. The key to a fruitful harvest, plentiful with abundance, safety, security, wealth, fulfillment, love, joy, the things most of us crave, is to be in a constant state of healing. I will provide strategies, along with anecdotes, of how I became the woman I am today. These strategies uncover how healing my mind, body, and soul continues to propel my life trajectory. They can, without a doubt, work for you too.

I envision healing of the mind, body, and soul as a trifecta. Sure it is possible to have one without the others, but in order to achieve true harmony, you want to have synchronicity between the three.

The Mind

Our minds can be our greatest asset or our greatest hindrance, often times, it is both. There are thousands of self-help books on how to master your own mind. Without truly developing introspection, I mean dwelling with your innermost thoughts, you leave your life to random chance (and that's kind of scary when you think about it).

1. Discover your purpose and act on it.

   I like to think of my purpose as my center. It is what I return to when I need to be reminded of why I'm really here on this Earth and who I'm supposed to serve. Many people describe living while unaware of their purpose like freefalling, I see it more as driving without a GPS. You're bound to make so many wrong turns, sudden stops, and sharp turns. I also see living without a purpose like driving without a GPS because it also impacts other people. You are on this Earth to help somebody. Plain and simple. When you aren't living in your purpose you're bound to get in more arguments, have random spurts of fussiness, and miss important deadlines and events, all because you didn't want to use directions. Every part of your life should have a purpose. Your friendships, your relationships, your career path, all of it. Anything that does not align with it, you should really think twice, really three times, before you explore it. That isn't limiting, it's intentional.

2. Pinpoint your kryptonite and address it head on.

   Everybody has a kryptonite. You know, like the point of weakness, so debilitating, that it could take even Superman down. No matter how hard you try, it's the one thing you just can't shake. That is the very thing preventing you from living your best life. For some people, it's physical food, alcohol, sex, or even another person. For others, it's invisible, but very real like laziness, shame, or fear of judgement. Recognizing your kryptonite should be instinctive because there are likely thousands of times its really messed your life over. If you can't think of yours, it just may be narcissism (look, somebody had to tell you). My kryptonite is perfectionism. I was raised to do good work, with good intentions and sometimes, when I feel like I'm not able to do my best, I don't do anything at all. That's the thing about your kryptonite, one minute, it can have you feeling like you're on top of the world and the next it can have you sinking in quicksand.

The Body

I love having career in health and medicine. Holistic healing is a large part of my purpose, which is why I simply want to encourage you that it is never too late to give your body the care it deserves.

1. Stop with the slander.

    We say some cruel things to ourselves. I mean words we wouldn't dare say to someone else, let alone aloud because we know how downright pitiful it truly is. Some of the worst things we say to ourselves are about our bodies, criticizing our shape, our height, our weight, our skin blemishes, our functionality or lack thereof. Your body is strong, and it is one of the best examples of what it's like to be unstoppable. Your body has quite literally carried you, and maybe even your children, through unspeakable moments of courage, of sadness, of laughter, and more. See your body for what it truly is, a machine. If it's not feeling or looking what you think can be its best, it's up to you to fix it.

2. You only get one, so take care of it.

    We spend a lot of time lying to ourselves. Making excuses, saying why we can't start taking care of our bodies, or why it's complex to make changes. Notice I've been saying we this entire time because wellness is a lifestyle. Although I'm fit and healthy, I think there are always ways to improve how we care for our bodies. Only you have the power to create the change you want to see from your life and body.

The Soul

Our soul is what makes us unique. It encapsulates our personality and essence, who we really are. Part of becoming unstoppable is knowing your soul is in good hands. I'm a Christian, but regardless of your particular religion, knowing God, His Angels, the Spirit, and His universe are guiding and protecting you brings an unimaginable comfort and safety. Literally, as I'm writing this, I'm on a plane flying alongside the most severe lightning I've ever seen in my life. I mean, multiple flashes per second, just lighting the sky with white light (sorry mom and dad!). Instead of feeling scared, I'm just writing this chapter, awestruck with the beauty and magnitude of nature. I don't know the first thing about safety precautions while witnessing a lightning storm from 39,000 feet in the air, but I know that I'm going to make it to my destination safely. Similarly, when you can rest in quite literally, the storms of life, with a peace, knowing that you are safe and things will be okay, even when you have no clue HOW they will work themselves out, then you are on the way to truly being unstoppable.

The previous strategies simply create the foundation for what I've used to become an unstoppable woman. True healing starts within and radiates out. This process happens each and every day. Unlearning bad habits and adapting better ones, surrounding yourself with people that support you and have your best interest at heart, choosing to do what's necessary to fuel your mind and body. Your harvest awaits, all you have to do is start planting.

Pam Kurt

Professional Women's Life Coach/Attorney

https://www.linkedin.com/in/pamela-kurt-41a26ba

https://www.facebook.com/Best-Version-You-103772311530954

www.BestVersionYou.com

www.PamKurt.com

Ms. Kurt as an attorney and business owner have won many awards and honors as well as held multiple Leadership Roles in her community. She has found a new passion. Her passion is to support and to empower women to be the best they can!

The most personal enjoyment is when her clients find their own way. Ms. Kurt has also a private professional women life coaching practice. BE THE BEST VERSION of YOU! This is an opportunity to elevate professional women to be the best version of themselves. Dream Believe and Achieve is her signature coaching program. Her coaching program has allowed her clients on a powerful self-discovery journey. She is currently accepting new private coaching clients. Please contact her at BestVersionYou.com to start your journey to become the BEST YOU.

For Everything There Is a Season

By Pam Kurt

"There is a time for everything, and a season for every activity under the heavens: a time to be born and a time to die; a time to plant and a time to uproot; a time to kill and a time to heal; a time to tear down and a time to build; a time to weep and a time to laugh; a time to mourn and a time to dance; a time to scatter stones, and a time to gather them; a time to embrace, and a time to refrain from embracing; a time to search, and a time to give up; a time to keep, and a time to throw away; a time to tear, and a time to mend; a time to be silent, and a time to speak; a time to love, and a time to hate; a time for war and a time for peace."

-Ecclesiastes 3: 1-8.

As I write this, I find myself reflecting on my own life. Am I actually unstoppable? How do you become unstoppable?

I believe each of us are unstoppable! We each have God-given gifts to use and hone through whatever life throws at us. For most of us, becoming unstoppable can be a struggle and even a lifelong quest to achieve.

As you look at your life, where were your seasons? Your times of Joy? Times of Conflict? Sorrow? Happiness? When I ask clients about these seasons and specific times of intense emotions, whether happiness or grief, the responses are usually major life changes or events they share with me. These events are usually associated with a strong emotion, like the birth of a child, graduations, marriage, promotions at work, new house, reaching goals. All of those events usually bring up positive and happy emotions. I try to bring them to that time again and reflect, what made that moment *matter?* Who did you want to be inside that moment? These are anchor points you should think of often, if not daily.

When we do experience joy, it is important we don't forget to allow ourselves to experience gratitude for those moments.

So, what if during the various seasons, it is not a happy one? There are inevitably seasons of grief, pain, sadness, or shame. A tragedy happens. A trauma occurs that we couldn't foresee or control. Someone leaves us, hurts us or even passes away.

Even in these moments, there are still reasons to find gratitude. I try to help my clients to maintain that sacred space of gratitude. Pain purifies our thankfulness in ways joy rarely does.

When was the last time you chose to be thankful for breathing? Walking? To be able to sit at a table with family?

Even the most difficult seasons in my own life-death, divorce, abuse, abandonment, financial struggles, fighting, the feelings of "not good enough" or unworthy of being loved- these brought me to a place of doubt and unhappiness. But "everything under the sun" exists in balance. There were lessons and opportunities in those moments, and there's a time for those things as well. It's very hard to see the lesson or the "why" while you're in it. Sometimes we can only simply get through to survive.

It is in these seasons, however, we find a reason to keep moving forward, and it becomes vital to find something in that season for which you are grateful. I'll be blunt, some of my seasons weren't great and sometimes I could only hold on to the fact that I refused to give up. I didn't come this far to only come this far. I tried to be positive and rest in the fact I knew this season would pass.

As you are going through those "not so good" seasons, have you ever hit the point where the only thing you can find to be grateful for is the fact you're breathing?

Sometimes we have to be grateful for the obvious, especially when all else feels hopeless. If you have a pulse, you still have a purpose! We can get through! Find that little gem of gratitude and hold onto it like a precious jewel.

When we experience seasons of pain, it opens our eyes to the small things we constantly take for granted. For instance, you may notice in many of my social media posts, I feature water. I cherish being close to the water and nature. Some of the most amazing moments in my life have happened near water, like my wedding. Or choosing to start my own private practice.

As time ticks on, you realize there are some of those moments available daily as well. You see a bird, a butterfly, maybe even a leaf, and pause to realize how perfect it is. Or you watch the rain hit the petals on a flower. When you practice gratitude, no matter the season, you can be aware of the joy, peace, and beauty around you daily.

For me, my moments of radiant joy include the birth of my son, raising him, and having those "mommy and Joshey" moments (his name is Josh).

Yet, I had so many doubts. It's easy to minimize those doubts and fears when we look back, but it's important to acknowledge they are there, rather than unfairly judge our present by a skewed view of the past.

It is important for me to remember those times of transition were getting me through to the next season. As a single mother, I worked any and all jobs to get through college and pay the bills. It was a difficult season full of worry, pain, conflict, and lack. There were times I just wanted to give up. I was exhausted and doubted myself and every decision I made. Yet, like so many of you, I kept going. Why?

When I just couldn't do it anymore, when I wanted to give up so badly, I would think about my son and my family. I wanted God to use me in any season to show my son YOU CAN GET THROUGH and YOU CAN achieve your dreams. Perseverance and determination work with God's help. Now, in reflection, I can see all of those struggles were worth it. When it seemed never-ending, it really was only a season.

When I reflect on my relationship with Josh's father, I am aware of another season of grief. We were married young, and then divorced when my son was quite young. The relationship was abusive and the scars had lasting effects. Emotionally, I allowed those scars to exist for years, and they haunted me. It led to more self-doubt and lack of self-confidence.

My tipping point was the knowledge I wanted my son to grow up in a strong positive household. It became apparent that it was more important than having a male in the home. That decision was so tough, yet this season brought me closer to God and my faith. I am a survivor and I am STRONG. This season showed me I could get through. When I embrace who God made me to be, I am unstoppable. It also allowed me to show my son the strength and respect that he wouldn't have received if I had chosen to stay in my marriage.

Because I was on a one-person income, of course there were tough times financially. I remember playing "eenie meenie miney mo" with my bills to figure out which one would get paid, because I couldn't afford to pay them all. I would pay the gas bill one month and the electric the next month and minimums on any credit cards. We experienced our utilities being shut off and the sense of lack. I became a master of "robbing Peter to pay Paul". During this season, to say we struggled was an understatement. There were times I didn't have enough change to make the quarter we needed to dry my son's clothes at the laundromat. I literally took Josh's pants and put them on the back of the chair by the heat vents to dry and when it wasn't finished drying by the morning, I used a hair dryer to finish them off so he could wear them to school. This season taught me to be resourceful and determined. It also hardened my resolve to not let my son experience lack like that again.

Even after I made it through school and began working, there were still times of self-doubt. I had scholarships, awards, and now my degrees! Yet, there were many times I still doubted myself and abilities. I felt embarrassed because of my past struggles or if I didn't fit in. Does anyone else struggle with their inner mean girl?

Who am I as a struggling single divorced mother? I struggled with the question of if I should even be an attorney, even after I busted my butt to graduate law school!! Was I good enough?

I questioned my path and all my decisions. What I realize now, is that God was showing me what I was called to do, not what I thought I was *supposed* to do.

Sometimes, the weight of our own expectations of ourselves is the heaviest burden we carry.

Once I passed the bar exam, I still taught at college and local schools. I taught at a local college and was also a substitute teacher in the local school district. I had so much fear I couldn't make it, I was scared to make any kind of commitment.

I was terrified to sign a lease for my law office. The amount was a car payment! and if I had already struggled to make it through just school, how could I afford my own business?!?! My pen shook so badly writing my name, it was nearly illegible.

If this was the opportunity that presented itself, then by God, I was going to go for it! I would leap off that cliff and fly or die trying.

One day I remember when I was driving to class, praying, "God am I supposed to be a teacher or lawyer?".

That day, the phone rang and rang at my law office. It grew and grew, until I had to start hiring interns and paralegals and sought out assistance with an additional attorney. Ultimately, I finally allowed myself to stop substitute teaching and only taught at the college in the evenings. There was so much uncertainty.

I'm not going to pretend I liked this season, I *hated* it. There was so much uncertainty, and I was still finding my feet, but I can see now this season was preparing me for greatness! To be the best me!

In the past 13 years since I opened my first law firm, there have been business struggles with partners, employees, and more. There have been unhappy clients and personal and professional attacks I would have never dreamt would occur. I was, and am, resolved in who I am, and I will prevail. (At least that's what I kept telling myself through those seasons.) It really does work out. Never as I expect, but God leads me usually to a better ending than I could have imagined.

In some of these painful seasons, I have experienced betrayal from close friends and family, addiction, abuse, and so much more.

I struggled with wanting to immediately jump in and fix it for these people by sharing my story. Yet despite encouragement, problem-solving, or opportunities, a person continues to choose to self-destruct. These experiences remind me to be grateful for what I know. Grateful for the opportunities. It taught me to understand I can't "fix" anyone, it has to be their own choice. I can support someone, but not at a sacrifice to myself. That delicate balance and power struggle is yet another lesson from those seasons. One of the miracles of gratitude is it gives us the energy to pass on what we've learned!

I have learned so much about me, and I've seen how God has provided! So many of my friends have heard me say, "I work without a net." I don't have a rich family or a rich husband. I built everything I have with my own hands and through hard work. The seasons of planting, and watering, before I could see anything resembling a harvest taught me the respect and ability to support others. You can have what you dream.

I want to be that person for those who doubt. I have been there and done it! Maybe I am the ultimate optimist, maybe I'm slightly crazy, but what I do know for sure, is if you are reading this or have come into my life, it's for a reason.

I try to look for the little things daily, to take a moment and truly see things. Life is precious and everything has a season. Try to enjoy and take note, as the times are only seasons you're passing through. They are temporary. Not meant to last. Enjoy and be grateful for the moment, because you won't have it again.

As I have mentioned, every day now isn't perfect. I do own several businesses, my own house, a nice car, my son is grown, I found true love, but I have learned it is all on God's timing, His season. There is a **reason and purpose for everything**. Sometimes we don't know the "why" but when you're given the opportunity, have gratitude that you get to see the reason on this side of heaven.

I am so grateful to see these lessons I've learned so far play out in my life. I know there will be more to come. So even though I won't admit I am getting "older," my life has been fulfilling and wonderful! I have experienced and been privileged to help more people than I could have ever imagined. These perspectives I have earned can't be taught in school. Those seasons have led me to be the best version of me. Those seasons I hated prepared me to be grateful and joyous. This has allowed me to be unstoppable.

Here's to a great future! You can't say the sky's the limit when we put footprints on the moon! WE ALL CAN BE UNSTOPPABLE! Dream. Believe. Achieve.

Alicia Marcos Birong

Guided Choices Inc Founder & Owner

https://www.linkedin.com/in/alicia-marcos-birong-4716177

https://www.instagram.com/guided_choices

https://www.facebook.com/guidedchoices

https://www.guidedchoices.org/pediatric-life-coaching

https://www.guidedchoices.org

Alicia Marcos Birong is a pioneer in the field of child mindfulness, speaking on the same stages with Mother Theresa and Pope John Paul II.

As the founder of Guided Choices, Alicia's signature programs have gathered national attention for their transformative abilities of children.

ChatterGirls™ offers in-person, hands-on guidance for 8-14 year old girls. Pediatric Life Coaching™ instructs parents, teachers, and coaches how to effectively help children overcome their daily hurdles.

Alicia's best selling book "Changing the Chatter" assists young girls in developing life skills for becoming strong, confident women.

A recipient of McHenry County Hero's Award, Alicia's passion for empowering children is evident. With 25+ years of experience as a therapist, counselor, life coach, and hypnotherapist, Alicia shares her expertise with communities across the country. You may have seen her on national television or working alongside companies such as Coca-Cola, Girls Scouts of America, American Express, and the YWCA.

Success Begins At Childhood

By Alicia Marcos Birong

Looking at some old home videos from my childhood, we all looked happy and like a normal family. My mother looked beautiful and had a beautiful smile on her face. But I recognized that smile and knew that it hid all her pain and loss. I too, would pull out the same smile, especially as an adult, when my own pain got to be too much. When a fake smile was all that was needed, it was an easy way to hide what was really going on in my life and in my head. The worst part was not realizing how much power each fake smile took away from me. I couldn't show how I was really feeling. I was sabotaging myself.

Throughout my life, I struggled with survival, and I sabotaged my success. In fact, as a child, success was not a word in my vocabulary. My childhood was lonely, fearful and loaded with failure. It was merely a place where I existed. While many children face hardships, mine began at home with my own mother's pain.

Around age 14, her life crumbled as the knowledge of her sister's molestation from their father came to light. By age 18, my father had left our family and my mother attempted to commit suicide. This sparked a conversation with her that brought out all the painful details from her childhood. While the knowledge of my mother's past did help me understand why she wasn't capable of being a good mother, the pain from not having a present and nurturing mother was still there.

Later on in her life, my mother was diagnosed with Schizophrenia, and she continued to live her life smoking, chugging coffee and sitting in front of the television. That was a typical night for me. She was there, but she wasn't there at the same time. It was a consistent sight to see my mom unaware of what was going on around her as the TV glowed. My dad would usually appear late in the evening expecting mother to have done something but that did not happen. If things needed to get done like dinner and household chores it fell on me. Since I really had no role models except my Aunt, I did the best I could. He had grown up in a house where his mom took care of the household chores and he expected it to be done by mom and when it was not there would be a lot of fighting and screaming matches with my mom. I understand today how my dad really did not have the tools to raise a daughter and as much as he loved my mom he could never change her. She was sick so he left and it was up to me once again. This time my life was put on hold. At 18 I took care of my Mom and brother.

School was the one place that allowed me some solace away from home. I attended a Parochial Catholic school through High School and struggled immensely with studying and homework. My classmates made fun of me for never having my homework turned in.

I was poor at studying and spent most of my classes seated next to the Sisters running the classes. What I never told anyone was that I never had time for these things because I was too busy taking care of my brother and what time I did have for homework was spent trying to figure out what I was looking at. Unbeknownst to me, I was struggling with Dyslexia but wouldn't receive a diagnosis until college. My home was dysfunctional and not safe, but I never told anyone until I was an adult.

School would've been a lot worse, if not for one of my favorite Sisters. She would always take time to sit and talk with me and remind me that I am a child of God and loved deeply by Him. Her care always stuck with me, and was a big part of giving back to children later in my life. If children don't receive love, concern, appreciation, or undivided attention from adults, it can severely affect their mental state. When their mental state is not set to accept how to be successful, they'll spend their lives sabotaging themselves much like I did.

Maybe it was the kindness of the Sister. Maybe it was something else but I decided to stick around the Catholic environment for my adult life. That decision changed my life. In 1983, while working at a parish outside of New Orleans I met Saint Mother Theresa. The moments with her were short, but She saw through my smile. The fake smile I had gotten away with throughout my childhood was not the smile she saw. She saw it, but she also recognized there was more to me hidden underneath. She looked into my eyes and told me to "Let it go". Let it go, all of it. My childhood, my poor parenting, my inability to choose a healthy life partner. I needed to let all of it go to free myself from the weight of my past. My children were my life and I loved them deeply. I wanted their lives to be different from mine and to know what a healthy home looked like. I needed to stop sabotaging myself and start making choices that were healthy for all of us.

What did sabotaging look like? Well, it was different at different parts of my life.

Sometimes I would be very successful, but I would feel like success couldn't be everywhere in my life at the same time. I never felt fully in control, so even though I was divorced, I let my ex back in. This was a mistake that could've cost me my life. I would spend my days serving as the Executive Directors of treatment centers. This meant I was in charge of helping to empower women, yet at home my ex was trying to kill me. Other times I was not being the best mother I could be, following right in the footsteps of my mother.

All-in-all I needed to escape the sabotage. I needed to take the words of Mother Teresa and "Let it go." So, I got in my car and drove, not knowing where I was going. I just knew I had something more to give to the world, and I wasn't going to find that part of me on the same path that I was on.

Ending the sabotage wasn't easy, but it was a learning experience I now share with my clients and my colleagues. The first part was healing. The second part was helping others. They actually go hand-in-hand very well. The more people you can help, the more you can forgive yourself, heal, and move on. For me, they started out separate.

Healing from the inside can be as simple as removing your everyday pressures. Find a happy place or find a calming place where you can reflect. Sometimes, you might reflect on the past and just recognize that you don't want that to be a part of you anymore. Other times it's thinking about the future. It allows you to escape and become a different person than you were yesterday.

For me, I lived with a friend, took a job with a catering company as a sales person, and was a barista at the beach at night. I found water to be my happy place, so I would walk on the beach everyday and reflect on what tomorrow could look like. This was only a year of my life, but it gave me the healing I needed so I could be ready to do more with my life, without the weight of self-sabotage.

When you are healed, the world opens up a bit more. New opportunities present themselves and you can play a bigger role in the life of others. This is when I found a passion for helping others. Actually, that passion was always there, but it wasn't until I was healed that I found a way to put my Masters of Counseling degree to better use. I went back to school and focused on hypnotherapy. Hypnotherapy was not a well-known counseling option at that time. In fact, at one point I was one of only ten in the entire country focusing on pediatric hypnotherapy. I took this niche market and I decided to start my own practice in Albuquerque and Santa Fe. My hypnotherapy teachers would send me clients and then students who wanted to learn the uniqueness of helping children with hypnotherapy. I was developing it more and more.

With each student helped, each child helped, I saw the impact of reaching children early.

The lack of success I felt in my childhood was not something I ever wanted another child to feel. I took it on myself to be more of an inspiration for others, so they never experience the life I had growing up.

Mother Teresa's words of "Let it go" continued to inspire and drive me towards new opportunities to help children. Sometimes it takes the most broken to know how to make the most progress with others. When you've been through it, you feel it. You see it with every child you talk to. You recognize the sadness behind the shyness or the anger behind the eyes. Broken homes, abuse, neglect, anxiety, PTSD, depression. These are the experiences of my life that millions of kids are dealing with every single day.

If they aren't given the tools to find the power inside of them, who knows how they'll view success or worse, find ways to sabotage their success like I did.

So, In 2000 I left Santa Fe, and headed to San Diego with my dog Koko. This was the first time in my life I was really on my own without another human being beside me. At this point my children were grown and living in Texas. There were no men in my life to serve. There was nothing left to stop my drive to help more people. Just the unknown and I lived with that my entire life.

I was no longer the little girl with no self-esteem. The shy child became a networker. I met people, made connections, and found opportunities. Within 2 months I had an office and lived at the beach overlooking the water. It was truly happening. The healing part of my life, water, and the helping part of my life, business, were coming together. Years ago, I would've thought this impossible.

There were some bumps in the road, of course. With every new venture, there are obstacles. Yet, the self sabotaging I'd experienced throughout most of my life was not controlling me like it had in the past. The techniques I used with children were also the techniques I used myself. Everyone experiences doubt. Discomfort. Insecurity. You name the emotion, and we've all experienced it. The key is to recognize the emotions and know they are normal, but not let them control you. Know that you have the power to be whoever you want to be.

In San Diego, I learned more about myself. I learned about Life Coaching and Neuro-linguistic Programming (NLP). With each lesson, I improved my business a little more and my own life a little more. I found new ways to coach my clients, and maybe most importantly, I also learned the value in helping more than one person at a time. All of this happened because of the impact that one person can have on another. My favorite Sister when I was a child. Mother Theresa when I was a lost adult. Without their impact, my Pediatric Life Coaching program and my ChatterGirls program would never have been born, and thousands of children would've been lost to self-sabotage.

Taking the lessons of my life, ChatterGirls gives girls aged 8-14 the opportunity to change the way they think about themselves. They have the opportunity to take a journey into their own mind and become that beautiful empowered young girl inside and out. It inspires the next generation of women and shows them how my journey wasn't the end. That program led to the Pediatric Life Coaching program, which teaches others how to show children the way forward. The more tools we can give others to impact lives, the more lives we impact as a whole collective. I started on my path solo, but that was only the beginning.

Since the growth journey began many years ago, I've given up the beach (my happy place) for my most supportive true love, my husband (my happier place). He is one of the most amazing people I've ever been lucky enough to have in my life. With all of the twists and turns along the journey, I've lived in 8 states and experienced powerful lessons from each location. I've met people in each state who have changed my life. I want to pass that onto others.

I am so grateful to know I have inspired many to follow their passion of serving others. While it may be painful at times, it's important to be willing to share your journey with your clients and inspire them to follow the path they choose. It's never easy to share pain. My experiences, especially as a child, were traumatizing but I know, hearing from young girls and women all over the country, that they are living in a shell of their full potential as well. They need to know they can be successful. They can be powerful. They can be unstoppable.

The shy girl in grade school now stands on stages with thousands of attendees, knowing that their own possibilities are within reach. They are always within. They just need guidance on how to take those unconscious thoughts and change them and make them a reality.

It's not where you came from or what sabotaging you did to destroy your journey, it is what you did to learn from the sabotaging. To know what people need and to be able to show that change can be good, even when it's scariest. I have changed but I do hold on to that image of the little girl I would often see in the mirror. That little girl cried, felt alone, and didn't view the world as welcoming. It was unempowering. The mirror showed the image of uncertainty. She is the image of the girl before she becomes the woman who could adjust to whatever she needs to.

I know. I see it every day with my daughter. She is such an amazing woman who has stood by me through it all. She is everything I was not at her age, a great mom, a successful businesswoman and wife. It took me a lot longer to find it than she did. Having a granddaughter made the issue right in my backyard. She's proof with the right support, love, and guidance that children can thrive.

As a child, I never saw success as possible for me. Now, I see that everyone's success is different. For some it might be money and for others it may be notoriety. For me, success was a gift that was inside me the whole time. My gift makes me unstoppable. It's the ability to help others see the value of their existence, the very thing I struggled with so many times before I heard the simple, most loving phrase "Let it go."

Nichole Riley-Simmons

CEO Credit Squad Inc.

www.Instagram.com/creditsquadinc

https://www.facebook.com/profile.php?id=100070033634581

https://creditsquadinc.com

My name is Nichole Riley-Simmons I was born in Manhattan New York. I moved to Savannah, Georgia with my father and grandmother. Since a very young age I was interested in reading and writing, it was definitely my strong suit. I have avidly read over 400 books throughout the years from different genres my favorite being nonfiction and romance novels. I slacked off from reading when I dropped out of high school my junior year to work full time. I went through many dead end jobs some I stayed for years until I started having my children and realized that I wanted so much more for them and myself (All detailed in my book Copied, Not Pasted! Available on Amazon) That is when I started pushing myself for the better. I still reside in Savannah with my 3 children Takeriona, Jumiek, & Jamir and Now the owner of Credit squad inc. and still going for everything else that life has for me.

Shattered But Not Broken

By Nichole Riley- Simmons

I spoke in my book Copied, not pasted about how I went from a regular 9-5 worker to a full time entrepreneur but here I want to be a little more transparent in hopes that my downfalls can be a guide of what not to do for ladies that fall in the same category as I did. After all there is no testimony without the test right? Well here goes. Surrounded by 4 walls, suffocating and scared wondering if this was really the life that I chose for myself, I sat in a 6 by 8 jail cell on the floor and promised myself if I ever got out of here I would make some changes.

I had now become a full blown statistic and I was utterly disgusted with my actions. The arresting officer wanted to let me go because he could tell that I wasn't the type to do what I was being accused of but he had to do what his commanding officer told him to do, and that was make an example of me for not telling on the person that actually committed the crime, so to jail I went. Shaking my head I wondered "How did I get here?" As my father used to call it, I was gullible. I had let a man trick me out of my freedom and my clean record. It's something that a lot of people don't know about me. I'm not a troublesome person at all but low and behold here I was 19, a high school dropout, and now a felon of a crime that I didn't even commit.

A complete failure. I didn't know how to even begin to put my life back together but I was going to give it everything that I had. After 4 days 7 hours and 32 minutes I was released. I had to mentally prepare myself for the 3 years of probation that I had to complete in order to get my record expunged. I ended up only doing a little over a year with supervised visits and the rest un-supervised. I knew and understood the struggles of finding what I wanted to do with my life and also having a record looming in the shadows, my options were limited. What could be worse than someone who lacks all of these things? a procrastinator. Yes, with all the things that I already had counting against me I had the gall to procrastinate with things that I could be doing.

There were jobs and opportunities that I could've had that I dragged my ass on and let slip through my fingers. I had scholarships, trade school and job corp recruiters wanting me but still and yet I was lost. I didn't know what I wanted to do with my life, all I knew was that I didn't want to have to depend on anyone. That was the one thing that kept me going. Fast forward to 2019 I had a slew of jobs, 3 kids, and so many bills that I couldn't even fathom being debt free. I had just become the average check to check worker just to provide my babies with a roof over their heads and clothes on their backs.

I was working so much I barely had time to bond with them and when I did I was tired and irritable. Something had to give. I prayed that God would give me a sign of what I needed to do. Out of nowhere came the answer. Ashley Massengill, Credit repair mogul, Serial entrepreneur, multi-millionaire amongst other hats that she wears. I stepped out on faith and took her spring 2019 training learning how to build a credit repair business from the ground up. When I took her class it put a fire up under me like no other. I learned about business, I formed business relationships and connections. I rebuilt my own credit profile and also helped some friends and family with theirs.

Alyson MacLeod

Founder & CEO Soul Expression Sessions

https://www.linkedin.com/in/alyson-m-macleod-25111a9

https://www.instagram.com/alyson_macleod

https://www.facebook.com/alyson.macleod1

https://www.facebook.com/groups/975044462903717

http://www.soulexpressionsessions.com

Alyson MacLeod, CHC is a Best Selling Author, Speaker, Serial Entrepreneur and Transformational Results Coach certified in Health, Life and Business Coaching. She has a degree in Community, Economics and Social Development but her greatest accomplishment is being the mother of 2 beautiful souls. She coaches Executive and high achieving Entrepreneurial Women who have lost their drive to succeed, find confidence again to Live their Destiny by refocusing, gaining clarity and learning to live in their full Soul Expression.

You will find the Soul Expression Sessions on the Wealthy Women Entrepreneur Network!

The Conquering Goddess: Embracing The Power Within

By Alyson MacLeod

Being Unstoppable is every little moment, step by step that brings you to another outcome. It is every decision that you keep making that moves you toward a goal that you envision. When you believe with all your heart that you are going in the right direction and no one or nothing can stop you from realizing your goal, the magic happens. It is in that moment that you catch momentum and your dreams start to become realized. You have embraced the power within you!

What if the bottom just falls out and the dream seems lost? In that moment you build resilience because being unstoppable means you are willing to live through the ups and downs, the trials and tribulations of life. No one builds self-confidence or self-esteem by sitting pretty and not getting their hands a little dirty or their hearts a little broken. We learn to adapt to situations and things that do not break us and we are willing to stand up and be accountable for everything in our lives, no matter what. You don't start out this way, you grow this way!

I left home at 18 years old. Good little catholic girl and very naive. My mom sent me away with a couple that didn't even like me. We had to stay on top of a gas station north of Toronto because their house wasn't even ready yet. I recall standing on the corner of Dundas and Yonge Street at the Eaton Center one day and I was wearing a short muskrat fur coat and just got my nails done. I looked and felt amazing. Everyone was honking at me and waving. I thought this was the friendliest city ever. Then the police pulled up and asked me what I was doing. I told them I was new to Toronto and it was nice here. Then I found myself in the back of a police car getting a ride home. They explained that what I was doing seemed more like looking for a date than enjoying a friendly city. I was mortified to think they thought I was a hooker. I don't know what happened to that coat but it definitely did not make it to the next winter and my friendly wave was no more, especially on street corners. Geesh!

The next 6 years were a very dark time in my life. I was raped by the brother of my ex-boyfriend, beaten by my boyfriend and left for dead. The police said I would be put on trial and they scared me into forgetting about it. I buried these terrible times as far down as I could and walked away from that life. I have not written these words nor have I told anyone about it since then but I have come to understand that these times defined who I became but not who I was.

By that I mean I can see how they tore apart every shred of love I had for myself and others but I also leaned in to find God inside of the chaos and that is what got me through. Prayer and meditation was the start of my healing. It became about me and not them. This was my first step into my healing journey that never ended until 35 years later when I was in a university class talking about intersectionality and personality traits when half the class burst into tears and we all needed therapy. I guess burying the past never stays there and needs to be dealt with. That was 2 years ago and I have to say that telling a therapist what had happened and why the class brought it out of me was enlightening and uplifting. I was finally feeling free and that made me feel unstoppable even more, like there was no more kryptonite that could stop me from achieving my goals. I finally felt worthy and empowered and very very light all of a sudden. I felt like I could fly.

I felt like this was a miracle that I needed and it came out of the blue. I love it when that happens!! So, I started to learn how to dig up what lies beneath my soul. I realized each experience, big or small, has consequences because of what we were told growing up. I've done some rapid transformational hypnotherapy that allowed me to go back to my childhood and see what was said to me. I needed to know why I was attracting certain situations into my life and why. I was always told that I would be married with children and take care of my husband and kids. I was never told I was going to have a career that made me a multiple 6 figure income. I do remember my dad, Papa Dorn telling me I could be whatever I wanted to but that little voice in my head told me I was not. Other times when I was told money does not grow on trees, quit wasting it or that I was not good enough to get something really struck a chord in my heart. It explained a lot when it comes to business, money and love (or lack thereof!).

I have to say that I am a constant learner and learning more about different modalities was a Godsend for me in searching for why I am how I am. Another notable thing about me is that I have ADD, I have had 2 hip replacements and a complete hysterectomy (with a bilateral oophorectomy) at the age of 43. So, finding out that I have a 133% higher chance than any other female to lose my marbles over 70 and forget my life gave me a little chuckle. Anyone who knows me understands that I research everything and will defy the odds! What else can I do, right? I feel unstoppable!

Unfortunately, bad things did happen to me on many occasions with and from people I trusted. It did not break me and today I stand tall. I know I am stronger than I thought and better than my circumstances. It was in those dark moments and spaces that I thought I was alone, so very alone. A wonderful little old lady I met at Women in Crisis came up to me with a big smile, gave me a huge hug and turned to say, "Now pick up your boot straps honey, this won't kill you but wallowing in it will." I was dazed and confused for quite a while. I told her I was fine and that I was not abused and she turned again and said, "Sweetie, he did everything but hit you where I could see it". I sat in her office and cried for the next hour. Then I got myself up, dusted myself off, dried my eyes and made a decision that day to never let myself be that cornered, abused and controlled ever again. She was an angel sent by God to make sure I was hugged and left with a sense of self that did not implode. I thank her every day for giving me a little kick in the butt and allowing me to grieve a little before standing tall.

I believe it is in these moments that we realize that we are stronger than we think and the world is wide open to whatever we want it to be. I could do whatever I wanted to but I believed I couldn't be successful without a husband period. Interestingly enough, I just had 2 decades of a very successful career in computer software sales and owning two gyms. I was a muti-6 figure earner for years.

We tend to revert back to our childhood beliefs and our self-confidence dissolves. I was a shell of a person for a very long time. My boys were always telling me how amazing I was and that one day I will be a millionaire. They are my biggest supporters and cheering section. I love them dearly! There were also a lot of people who I looked to for that support and it just was not there. I am finally in a place where I do not need other people's approval or support for my goals to be achieved. I have an amazing tribe of women who love and support what I do and who I am doing it for. So, if you are seeking approval to stop, you are amazing right where you are, a loved and cherished beautiful lady.

In 2020 I stopped being a business and health coach to really find out where God wanted me to go and do. I enlisted the help of a friend who was a coach and began the journey of finding me. It was scary to think that after 40 years of working I needed to find myself. I didn't even tell anyone because I was so embarrassed. Then I met some amazing women along the way going through the same thing I was. We worked together and as the saying goes, you help yourself when you help others! I found me!!!

I realized that I was unstoppable all along and that resilience is a big part of it and so is Love, Understanding, Compassion and Passion for all people and things. I knew I had greatness in me as a daughter of the most high King but it took a year of being contemplative to see what I can become. It was in those silent moments hearing the wind in the trees that would bring such clarity or the downloads during a meditation that God wanted everyone to know and hear. My inner self felt changed from fear to excitement and apprehension to action. I am taking action on what my destiny is and that empowerment and motivation comes from God. He has shown me who I am and how I can help other women who have experienced crazy situations in life.

One of the biggest lessons I learned so far in life is, ***if it is meant to be it is up to me***! Simple but true. Nothing I have ever done or thought of doing got accomplished unless I sat down, figured it out, took inspired action and did a lot of praying to get there. I followed God's direction and with the ease and flow there was success and if there was pain and impossible odds, then it was not meant to be and my ego was doing most of the work. That stopped me in my tracks. Not to say that nothing hard will come along, all are good lessons, but when everything does not feel right then reassess actions and motivations. High emotional intelligence is also key to living an Unstoppable life. I had to stop my ADD brain from going sideways during chaotic times so I could manage what was happening. It takes time to learn but we have the time, so use it wisely.

I had to learn that my daily mode of operation had to include several things to allow me to embrace the power within me. **My miracle zone** moments now begin with **gratitude**. It is essential that each day starts and ends with what I am grateful for. It sets up and ends my day in a peaceful, wonderful and joyous calm way that is all mine, and can be yours too. Try to make it a habit to write them out in the morning and see if you have new ones at night. The simple activity of writing them down allows your brain and physiology to react in a positive and calm manner.

I have also used **forgiveness** as my weapon of choice. The past cannot hurt me anymore as I have forgiven anyone who has hurt me and lifted them up to God. He can deal with them much better than I can, after all he does have all the world's resources at his disposal. Forgiving myself was the hardest one though. After taking full responsibility for all the good and the bad, I felt sad, anxious and depleted but that did not last because I knew that forgiving myself allowed me to move on more powerfully and on purpose than ever before. If it is meant to be it is up to me and I could not have a little thing like unforgiveness stop me.

I had to forgive every bit of me from my head to my toes which took a while but now I am ready to kick butt and take names. Bringing on the next chapter of my life is exciting and transforming now!

Compassion is what I give every day to those around me. I have learned to slow down and see everyone for who they are and where they are at. The last 2 years have put the fear of everything into people's hearts and with a little love and compassion we can help free people from those wounds.

Loving kindness also helps those wounds heal. It makes people feel like they matter and that they are worthy. I give some time to those who just need me to listen for a while or have me show up for tea on their birthday. It goes a long way to lift someone up and make them feel better. It makes me feel happy and purposeful too.

Generosity is a big one for me. I believe that if I have something I do not need or am not using any longer why hold on to it. Share it!! I supported several causes as a 6 figure earner because they were for children or the elderly in my community. You can also volunteer for a couple hours a week or a month and it will make all the difference in the world.

Prayer and **meditation** I do daily along with **stretching** (yoga). My health depends on it. My Soul loves to express itself with a calmness and radiance that people feel when shared. You are a Goddess and staying grounded and centered is your birthright. Claim it!

So what does your miracle zone look like? Make sure it encompasses YOU in it too. It has to feed your soul!! Self-Love and compassion for yourself goes a long way to keeping your Unstoppable and kryptonite free world. Each day is a great day and whatever happens, you will be stronger, happier, resilient and UNSTOPPABLE!

Remember that nothing outside of you will fulfill you if you do not embrace the power and love that emanates from within you. Your joy can never be measured by someone else or by the feeling that you are doing it right or by anything outside of YOU! You are Unstoppable inside and out! *May you find Pure Love inside the sanctuary of your precious heart! - Alyson MacLeod*

Blessings

XOXO

Jennifer Cairns

Lead Rebel @ Lady Rebel Club® & The Brand Evolution Expert

https://www.linkedin.com/mwlite/in/jennifer-cairns

https://www.instagram.com/lady.rebel.club

https://www.facebook.com/LadyRebelClub

https://www.brandevolutionacademy.com

https://in.pinterest.com/BrandEvolutionAcademy

I'm a mum, wife and neurodiverse, award-winning 4x entrepreneur who believes everyone is a goldmine and has value to share. I live in Northern Ireland with my husband, two boys and ball-obsessed dog Milo. I run Brand Evolution Academy, where I show service providers, creators and change-makers how to separate themselves from their businesses and overcome the personal branding myth that drags them down. instead, I show how to build the kind of kick-ass brand that skyrockets their confidence, their impact and their revenue.

I'm also creator of Lady Rebel Club, a community that aims to support, empower and advocate for women entrepreneurs who are neurodiverse and/or who have a hidden disability or disorder. Myself, I'm neurodiverse, have an extremely rare blood cancer, paraneroplastic syndrome, dissociative seizures, fibromyalgia, GAD and CPTSD.

Rise Of The Phoenix

By Jennifer Cairns

Awake fire. Awake.

As a kid, I seemed to have an inner grit; a string of light that held me together and helped me survive many things in my youth. Those were turbulent years that left many scars. Underneath all the turmoil, I started to become aware that I wasn't like other kids. The older I grew, the more apparent that became. Yet, the more I felt different, the harder I tried to fit in at first. Feeling the need as so many do, to be "liked", to fit in. Often finding myself going to extreme measures to prove that I was one of them.

Those childhood traumas layered over me, one poorly taped edge pulled tightly over another. Years passed and I grew up always knowing that the tape could come undone at any time and I'd be left open and exposed, my scars and fears laid helpless for all to see.

As my childhood gave way to my twenties, I drifted. Just like driftwood loses its roughness over time, my badly taped edges were sanded and moulded with every crash of a wave. The waves roared, and I learned to mask, to blend, and it became easier to hide. My masks held firm while internal storms raged, making it easier for me to make poor choices and fall prey to ill-intentioned people.

After many years of being tossed in the waves, my neatly sanded edges started to creak and crack. The layers I tried to hide, the storms and the "me" I didn't really understand started to put pressure on my damaged exterior. A crack turned into a split. That spilt widened, and my wave-polished wooden shell finally broke away. I was unprotected, unmasked and raw. Me, I thought I knew, the me that I didn't want to know, the me that held the hurt and scars of all those years laid at my feet like a pyre. All the "me's" and my masks were now kindling and as often happens, kindling started to flicker. Then the flickers turned to flames.

It wasn't my intention to awaken this sleeping superpower. The power that I wanted to run and hide from most of my life. It wasn't my intention to rise, gritting my teeth and staring at the pain, the scars, the me I didn't understand... but I did.

Although I still didn't understand *everything*, I couldn't name the power I'd been granted, yet now I knew I had it. Like a Phoenix must rage and burn and lose all of herself to be born from the ashes, I rose stronger and fiercer.

Let the waves come crashing, my fire can't be drowned.

As the years rolled by, life's waves still lapped at my ankles, letting me know that their wildness and power could not be tamed. I married a kind, caring and funny man and have been blessed with two lovely, spirited and amazing boys. Not forgetting our dog Milo, who my youngest considers more of a brother than a four-legged friend.

Over the years, I've had numerous struggles with anxiety disorders, dealing with the past, health, surgeries, two near-death experiences, 11 car crashes, bad and abusive relationships, lost businesses, lack of money and other hoops and hurdles that often plague most. Through them all, I survived.

Sometimes it was by the grace of God or the universe's magical plan, perhaps. Also, I was able to reach into myself and know that although I may lay shredded, weak or broken, although yes, waves will always come, I knew that I would rise and the waves would eventually calm.

A superpower can give you strength, courage, cunning, positivity, generosity, kindness, cleverness, ideas or something else just as wonderous. When waves roar and they will, we all have our own unique superpower that will flame and help us withstand the storms and appreciate the light. The trick is to look within. Listen, look, and you'll find it.

Plus, a sense of humour doesn't hurt.

When life sets your world to fire, you can sit roasting marshmallows, or you can walk through it and own the flame.

It really does seem in life things come in threes, often very close together or all at once.

Wave one:

In November 2019, out of the blue, my family was smacked by a life-changing event. My 42-year-old husband had a stroke. Just two weeks before, a huge programme we'd been building for months was due to launch and three days after routine gallbladder surgery. We were all shocked. He ran six days a week and was in great health.

We later found out that he had a tiny blood clot form after his surgery that went through a hole in his heart and up to his brain. None of us knew he even had a hole in his heart! We were all shocked and devastated.

Yet after the dust settled a bit and the shock wore off, my superpower kicked in and then I was thankful. Thankful he was alive. Thankful he'd be able to make some recovery. Thankfully he could walk, and after months of physio and hard work, he could fully walk. As he'd admit, his football days are over, but as we know, it could have been far worse.

The impact on him, on the kids, on the rest of the family and me, even on our business, was immense. I can't say it was easy because it wasn't but I called upon my superpower to pull things together. There was a lot to juggle, and it was far from easy, yet my grit and determination helped me rise.

Wave two:

A couple of months after his stroke, my husband was home from the hospital and was treated as an outpatient at the Brain Injury Unit. We were all adjusting to the new as best as we all could when I was sent for a bone marrow biopsy of my tailbone by one of the many doctors I was seeing. They'd seen something on a previous MRI. Though they thought it was a giant cell tumour... but at the end of January, the doctor told me those devastating words, "It's lymphoma."

The sea groaned and swelled up again, not completely settled from the previous wave. I was given a date to see a hematologist consultant and found out I have a rare blood cancer called lymphoplasmacytic lymphoma (LPL). It's pretty rare and out of that small percentage, nine out of ten cases are a type called Waldenstrom's but my type of cancer didn't fit neatly into its box either.

As I didn't fit neatly into one specific box, they've given my cancer its very own special name: lymphoplasmacytic lymphoma with MY88 protein without paraprotein. Yes, it's a mouthful! It turns out I'm the 1% of the 1%. My husband and I joke now, as I always tell him how special I am and that I have never fit into one neat box my entire life; why would this be any different!

Wave three - where they collide:

Covid.

This was hard on the world, not just us. I knew so many that were in terrible situations or had lost loved ones. For me, the hardest part was the effect it had on my kids, especially my youngest. That is his story to tell, or not tell, so I'll not say much about it except that it affected him terribly.

The other two biggest issues with Covid then were that it would likely terribly affect me, and I was grouped in the high-risk category. Ironically, that didn't make much of a difference during the hard lockdowns. It is and will play on my mind a lot more now with things opening up.

Because of the type of cancer I have, the vaccine doesn't offer much-added protection. While others are boosted to 90-95% or more, I'd be lucky to reach 20%. So as people mingle and kids are back in school, I do worry. I can't say I don't but we're cautious and mitigate risks as much as possible. The kids have been allowed the odd 'outing' with friends for their mental health, and so they can remember what being a kid should be about.

In five months, my husband had a stroke, I was told I have lymphoma, and the world came to a standstill with Covid. Yet even when I took treatment during the first lockdown, I seemed oddly calm to most people. I smiled more than most could understand and was thankful when people kept telling me how terrible it was on top of everything that had happened that I had cancer.

Was I any happy I had cancer? No. Did I wish I didn't have it? Yes.

I was grateful that it wasn't *worse*. For me, there was nothing that could happen worse than one of my kids having it, as most parents or caregivers would agree. I was happy to take all the pain, tiredness, sickness, dizziness, the spreading loss of feeling and intensifying nerve pain and seizures on the chin. I was able to tackle all the waves life had thrown because of my superpower.

I'd been reduced to ash so many times in my life, but nothing like what those five months reduced me to. I did collapse and wept and wondered, "Why?" but after those fleeting thoughts were burned by my superpower. My strength and determination flamed and soared like never before. I knew I had this hidden strength, a grit, that I called on when needed.

It was with me from the moment I was born. It will be with me until the day I pass. Nobody can take it from me, it is mine alone and unlike anyone else's superpower. You see, until I was in my mid 40's, I didn't know I was neurodiverse and when I found out, I smiled as it made perfect sense.

Being autistic made sense of me feeling different and often thinking differently than most of my peers. It made sense of all the "pretending", or masking, and of many other feelings and thoughts that I'd had my whole life. Most importantly, it allowed me to give my superpower a name.

I was grateful. Were there many times life could have been easier if I'd not been neurodiverse? Sure. But then, I wouldn't have the gift of this steel-like grit and determination. Being neurodiverse didn't stop waves from hitting me or falling to ash at times but it did help me flicker, then flame and rise even stronger.

I'm a Phoenix, You're a Phoenix, Everyone's a Phoenix!

If you're here reading my ramblings, firstly, thank you for sharing your time with me and allowing me to share a part of my world with you.

My life was, and in fact, usually is, a beautiful mess.

You don't need to be perfect, organized, happy, confident or strong all of the time. You'll sometimes cry, be pissed off, sad, and scared... yet you'll *still* have a superpower. My superpower ended up being my neurodiversity and the strength it gives me. It was with me for most of my life, and I didn't even know it.

Maybe like how I was for so long, you're unable to see what your superpower is. Yet I assure you it's there. It may come rushing out at times of turmoil, or it may slowly drip into your days. It's in you, and it's yours and yours alone.

Want help to find it? Ask others. What are the same words people say about you over and over again? How would you describe yourself? Journal to find hidden patterns or thoughts. You can also try personality type tests, though don't assume your superpower fits into that neat box. Also, look at what you do or how you are that make you feel good about yourself. Dig, and you'll find it.

While we're chatting, keep in mind that we never know what life will bring. Big waves, small waves and still waters will hit everyone at different times and in different ways. Someone who has millions today may also have ill health tomorrow. Someone who has great health today maybe lost their partner yesterday. Nothing in our lives is always completely bad or perfect. It all comes in waves. When your wave is still, someone else's may be raging.

This is why I say to myself, my kids, and to others when they need to hear it; there will always be someone who has it better and someone who has it worse to whatever situation you're in. Knowing that might not make your situation better, yet thinking about how much worse it could be, makes you feel grateful. Just knowing it could be better gives you hope.

Find your superpower. Make the most of the times when your seas are still and be grateful and hopeful when your seas have waves that crash and swell.

END.

Savannah Eileen

Owner Of Eileen Entertainment LLC

https://www.linkedin.com/in/saveileen

www.instagram.com/saveileen

www.EileenEntertainment.com

www.Eileenfloral.com

www.TheEileenFoundation.org

Savannah Eileen is a 22 year old Serial Entrepreneur from Las Vegas, Nevada. She is the CEO of Eileen Entertainment, a special events and floral company, and the founder of The Eileen Foundation, a Non-profit helping to build passion, perseverance, and hope in our future leaders.

Falling In Love With Failure

By Savannah Eileen

It is difficult to try to see something like failure in a positive light. We go our entire lives avoiding this feeling. Why should we change that? Why should we invite failure into our lives?

Failures are the "growing pains" to success. Each failure is a stepping stone closer to the end of the race. Falling in love with failure forces us to acknowledge how beautiful the journey really is.

THE BRIEF STORY OF CEO & FOUNDER SAVANNAH EILEEN

The mentality embracing failure rather than fearing it has transformed my life. In 2019, I went through what I thought was the biggest failure of my life. I dropped out of college.

My whole childhood my parents taught me the only way to achieve success or have anything to fall back on was to go to school. When I was 12 years old, I began my first business. When my mother informed me I would no longer be receiving an allowance, my thoughts immediately turned to how I was going to earn money. I placed the remaining funds on a prepaid card at the grocery store. I used this to buy little things on eBay or reselling apps. While on these apps I wondered "Could *I* sell things here?" Slowly, I began flipping items, selling old clothes and accessories, and even flipping cheap items I saw at discounted stores. It was my first time making money and it felt awesome. At 14, I began my second venture, Instagram flipping. When the algorithm was at its best, and hashtags performed miracles, it was possible to create Instagram pages with specific niches and resell them on eBay.

When high school came, I was accepted into a technical school. Of course, being in school only reinforced the idea that college was the only option. I began to consider what I wanted to study, but I had a hard time pinning down what curriculum I was most passionate about. I didn't receive the best grades in school. This made me feel as if I was a failure, but little did I realize I was not a failure and I was not "dumb." I had just not yet realized my passion and what my true purpose was.

After graduating, I went to college. This was the path everyone expected me to take. As time passed, I remember getting more and more 'burn out', sad, and just unpassionate about how I was learning. I concluded that I wanted to run my own business. I wanted to feel that thrill again. As a result, I established a clothing line by the name of SAVSEI. I recall working for a while, going to school full-time, and beginning this side business. I recognized that I felt most pleased when I was doing anything related to my business.

This business wasn't highly successful. I had fun and I sold clothes, but it wasn't enough to continue as a successful business. I could've easily seen this as a failure, but instead, I took it as a learning experience. This business showed me that becoming a business owner was my genuine calling.

Most of my family regarded my dropping out of college as a major failure, but I had decided to take charge of my life and pursue the clichéd goal of running a successful business. Looking back, this was the best thing that ever happened to me.

When the pandemic struck, my clothing line suffered greatly. At this time, I was also doing event planning on the side. I remember going through a difficult period in my life when the city was on lockdown, I was home alone, and I felt like a complete failure. I stopped promoting my clothes because too many people were losing their jobs and I wasn't interested in selling them anymore. There were no events to arrange with the event planning business. I considered returning to school, but I knew it would not make me happy. Little did I realize as I thought the world was ending, it was only getting started.

Eileen Entertainment began in my house in the middle of lockdown. I had some expertise with balloons, decorations, and a little floral from my side event business. As a result, I decided to start selling products rather than services. I'd lost a lot of money trying to keep my businesses afloat while also being laid off from my job during the pandemic. I used my last $500 to invest in the business I wanted to start. I went out and got products to make balloons and flowers, and when I started posting my creations they suddenly went viral out of nowhere. I made five figures in sales in two months, bought a cargo van, and was now looking for our first storefront.

Even during those two months, I had massive failures that I perceived to be disastrous.

I recall having numerous nights during the first six months of Eileen where I had complete mental breakdowns over financial, customer service, and leadership failures. There were countless moments when I wanted to give up, but I understood that this was part of the "growing pains of success" as I like to call it.

GROWING PAINS OF SUCCESS

Nobody prepares us to be wrong, lose, or fail. How many times does a real entrepreneur fail before achieving illusory success? The answer is many times, and from each one, they learn something.

The door of opportunity is there, it could be the 4th house on the block but most people will give up after the first few houses say no and shut the door. Some people won't even start because they're afraid of the 'No's that will happen. Not everything works out the first time. It is common for many failures to occur before achieving success. These failures reveal weakness, allowing for and demanding improvement. Making mistakes does not mean that you have failed. Failure teaches you more about the process, success, and ultimately, yourself.

So why are so many of us fearing and avoiding failure at any cost?

WHY DO WE FEAR FAILURE?

We want to avoid getting hurt, particularly from rejection. In avoiding failure, we deny ourselves the unique learning and experience that comes from growth and failure.

Failure hurts our ego.

Our ego makes us vulnerable at times and coping with failure seems like the worst thing that can happen to someone. It causes remorse, shame, and a loss of self-esteem. It's no wonder that people are terrified of failure. It's awkward, uncomfortable even. The harder you work for something, the more painful the failure will be.

Nobody likes to be in pain or to be humiliated. This is partly because we were taught to avoid failure and it was always used in a negative connotation. Some individuals are willing to abandon their ambitions to avoid feeling worthless and experiencing emotional anguish through failure. Fear is a decent excuse not to take the risks necessary to achieve success. Fear may be a good enough reason to avoid pursuing chances that do not guarantee a positive result.

But is this how you want to spend the rest of your life?

Consider this.

You have two options: live in fear and avoid difficulties or take a new approach to your life. One in which failure does not have such a bad connotation. A life in which you learn from your mistakes and emerge stronger than before after each setback. In this, the ego dies and the soul awakens.

HOW CAN FAILURE BE ACCEPTED AND SEEN AS A POSITIVE RATHER THAN A NEGATIVE?

The ability to capitalize on our failures is the key to success. Unfortunately, many individuals do not understand how to recover from their mistakes. Instead of choosing to persevere in their path toward success, they choose to quit.

The capacity to capitalize on the possibilities presented by failure is the crucial distinction between successful and average individuals. The secret to success is to take advantage of failure. Failure incites growth; in the business and yourself. Below are some points on how to view failure in a better light and make use of all that it has to offer.

THE BEAUTY OF FAILURE

- Teaching Compassion

  In failing, you may respond more emphatically to others, who fail you if you face certain losses yourself. From your personal experience, you know that nobody is unfailing and that failure occurs. So, if someone feels defeated, you are more inclined to forgive mistakes and empathize as a leader.

- Promoting Self Awareness

  Those who fail must accept responsibility for their actions. In most instances, you had a role in your failure. Self-reflection is essential in losses to learn from them and be successful in the long run. You may remember from your mistakes and improve your chances of success the next time you attempt.

If you take a risk, you will almost certainly fail at some point. This has happened to a plethora of successful people. Both Joanne K. Rowling and Stephen King were unable to find publishers for their works. Astrid Lindgren felt the same way about her novel "Pippi Longstocking." Steve Jobs was even dismissed from his own business.

All these people had one thing in common, though: they refused to be pulled down by their losses and instead, found the strength to go on. Below are some points for how to cope with failure:

COPING WITH FAILURE

- Embrace the Discomfort.

  First, you must acknowledge your defeat before you can cope with it. Embrace all the feelings that come with a setback including sadness, rage, despair, and disappointment. It stings to be defeated. You put in a lot of effort and it wasn't worthwhile in the end. You contributed resources that are now irreversibly lost. This may seem quite overwhelming, but you must release these feelings to overcome them. Seek advice from a friend or family member who encourages you to let go. After allowing your emotions to run their course, you will be able to look ahead once again.

- Analyze the Issue From a Neutral Standpoint.

  Only when you've let your emotions out should you begin to analyze the issue objectively. It is useless to dwell on self-pity or create self-doubt. Attempt to discover the root reasons for your failure. Several variables often play a part in a loss. As a result, the issue is complicated and requires considerable thought before you can completely comprehend it. First and foremost, concentrate only on the analysis. The only way to learn from previous mistakes is to recognize what went wrong so you can prevent it from happening again.

- Maintain Pride

As I have said, sinking into self-pity after defeat does not assist you. It doesn't make you feel better, and it doesn't make the situation any less dangerous. Maintain your confidence and attempt to see your loss as a fresh opportunity. It's not easy at first. However, after you've acknowledged your failure, you should try to find a way to make the most of a dire circumstance. Take credit for your actions, for taking the risk in the first place. Despite the dangers, you trusted in yourself, and not many individuals would dare to make this move.

- Solicit Feedback

Question yourself objectively. What are your strengths and shortcomings? What do you need to improve? What makes you unique? Make a list of these ideas and consider how to transform your weaknesses into your strengths. Perhaps you might research online or read a book on the topic to prepare yourself better again.

Ask your friends what they perceive as your strengths. When the inner critic is too loud, you may not even be aware of your qualities. Outsiders will be able to see your positive qualities more objectively. If you agree with these points of view, you will be able to capitalize on these advantages in the future.

- Be Inspired.

  After considering all of the issues raised, it is time to consider the future. You've now spent enough time delving into the past. You should now take another look forward. However, before you begin, you should carefully consider your options. Keep your strengths in mind and evaluate if they are a good match for your objectives. It is also helpful to take inspiration from other successful people, examine their histories, and use their experiences to influence yours. Perhaps this will provide you with a fresh perspective on your predicament. But always keep an eye on your situation and personality. Continuously assess how you should work in a corresponding case.

- Make New Goals.

  It also makes sense in certain instances to choose a different route. If your objectives no longer fit into your current life plan, it is time to consider a change. Perhaps your loss has shaken you to the core, and you know you need to alter direction. However, you should not do this just because you failed. If you quit now, you may regret it for the rest of your life.

  Allow your brain and intuition to speak for themselves: Do you still believe you're on the right track? Do you need a new target? It's time to make a decision. Stand firm in your choice and face the situation head-on. Once you learn to cope with failure and see it for what it truly is, you can succeed not just despite it, but because of it.

A GUIDE TO SUCCEEDING DESPITE FAILURE AND BENEFITING FROM IT

- Create a Plan B

  If you want to do something but aren't sure if it will work or fail, prepare a backup plan just in case.

  Your backup plan should contain all of your objectives and methods for accomplishing them. This technique will reassure you that if you fail, you will try again, reducing your fear factor in the process. It will also reaffirm your long-term objectives and motivate you to take action and get started again.

- Accept the Failure and Reflect

  Before or after it occurs, you must acknowledge failure as something that most, if not all, of us, experience. You need to recognize a failure's potential usefulness and avoid fear.

  The most important aspect of the process is spending a few minutes reflecting on what occurred and being brutally honest with ourselves about why it happened.

- Fail Forward

  Learn from your mistakes and make the necessary changes until you succeed. Each change that we make, each person we meet, contributes to a different result. We cannot prevent obstacles from arising in our lives, but we can choose how to deal with them.

- Remove Negativity from Your Life

You may be surrounded by those who want to bring you down and discourage your willingness to try again. At times they will probably say things like "I told you so" and "You're better off this way." However, if you desire something, don't allow the negativity of others to affect you. Ignore those who do not motivate you to be the best version of yourself.

The book mantra is

ORDINARY WOMEN DOING EXTRAORDINARY THINGS

Each chapter was authentically written and represents each author's journey and testimony on Becoming An Unstoppable Woman. If you are facing adversities, barriers, or insecurities of any kind then this book is for you! You will learn:

* To live a life without limits
* Find your purpose and passion
* Becoming a brave entrepreneur
* Never settling, always excelling

* The unstoppable mindset
* The art of letting go
* Collaboration over competition
* And so much more!

She Rises, She Leads, She Lives
Join the #BAUW Becoming An
Unstoppable Woman Movement
www.SheRisesStudios.com

JOIN THE MOVEMENT!

#BAUW

Becoming An Unstoppable Woman

With She Rises Studios

She Rises Studios was founded by Hanna Olivas and Adriana Luna Carlos, the mother-daughter duo, in mid-2020 as they saw a need to help empower women around the world. They are the podcast hosts of the *She Rises Studios Podcast,* the TV show hosts of *Becoming An Unstoppable Woman*, as well as Amazon best-selling authors and motivational speakers who travel the world. Hanna and Adriana are the movement creators of #BAUW - Becoming An Unstoppable Woman: The movement has been created to universally impact women of all ages at whatever stage of life, to overcome insecurities, adversities, and develop an unstoppable mindset. She Rises Studios educates, celebrates, and empowers women globally.

Looking to Join Us in our Next Anthology?

Becoming An Unstoppable Woman Entrepreneur

Visit www.SheRisesStudios.com to see how YOU can join the #BAUW movement and help your community to achieve the UNSTOPPABLE mindset.

Have you checked out the *She Rises Studios Podcast?*

Find us on all MAJOR platforms: Spotify, IHeart Radio, Apple Podcasts, Google Podcasts, etc.

Looking to become a sponsor or build a partnership?

Email us at info@sherisesstudios.com